Dr Xanthé Mallett is a forensic anthropologist and criminologist, TV presenter and author. Xanthé's first book, *Mothers Who Murder* (Penguin Random House, 2014), re-evaluated the evidence in a number of potential miscarriages of justice, and aimed to improve our understanding of how, when, and why women can be driven to intentionally hurt their own children. Her second book, *Cold Case Investigations* (Pan Macmillan, 2019), reviewed a number of open Australian investigations and highlighted new forensic techniques or knowledge that could help progress the cases.

Xanthé is also a forensic practitioner, and works with police forces across Australia assisting with the identification of persons of interest in criminal cases, as well as providing advanced DNA technologies that assist with the identification of long-term deceased persons and suspects.

In addition to her academic and professional work, Xanthé has contributed to various true crime television series, most recently *Murder, Lies & Alibis* on Channel Nine, and is a regular contributor to crime news stories for television, radio and print media.

T0322696

Also by Xanthé Mallett

Cold Case Investigations

REASONABLE DOUBT

Lost lives, justice delayed, criminals walking free: exposing Australia's worst wrongful convictions

DR XANTHÉ MALLETT

MACMILLAN
Pan Macmillan Australia

First published in 2020 in Macmillan by Pan Macmillan Australia Pty Ltd
1 Market Street, Sydney, New South Wales, Australia, 2000

 A catalogue record for this
book is available from the
National Library of Australia

Typeset in 12/16 pt Garamond by Midland Typesetters, Australia
Printed by IVE

For all those who have been falsely accused, their families, and others who have suffered due to failings of the criminal justice system. Your stories should not be forgotten.

CONTENTS

INTRODUCTION

'It is better 100 guilty persons should escape than that
one innocent person should suffer.'

Benjamin Franklin

Murder victims, sexual assault victims, victims of family violence. All of these and many more come to mind when we think about who is harmed by violent crime.

But victimisation can also occur at the hands of the system established to mete out justice when people break the law by falsely accusing innocent people; when this happens miscarriages of justice occur.

A miscarriage of justice is the failure of the judicial or court system to attain justice. There are many types of miscarriages of justice, one of which is a 'wrongful conviction', a term that relates to individuals who are factually innocent of the crimes for which they have been convicted. Wrongful convictions happen for many reasons, but common causes are false or coerced confessions, mistaken eyewitness identifications, lying witnesses, lack of disclosure, or poor professional practice by the police, legal counsel or forensic experts. Forensic evidence can also be contaminated, introduced

1

or misinterpreted, which can also lead to wrongful convictions. A combination of these can occur within one case.

The implications of these influences couldn't be more profound, not just for the person wrongly convicted, but for everyone, as we all want to have faith that our justice system is founded on fairness and transparency. Sadly, sometimes that simply isn't the reality.

Consider the infamous Birmingham Six case in the United Kingdom, when six Irishmen were sentenced to life imprisonment following their false confession to planting bombs in two Birmingham pubs, which killed 21 people and injured 182 in November 1974. This was the worst peacetime atrocity on English soil in terms of people killed and injured until the 7 July bombings – a series of coordinated suicide terrorist attacks in London in 2005, in which 52 people were killed (plus the four bombers) and a further 784 injured.

The men had links to the Provisional IRA, a terrorist organisation, which led to the police making assumptions about their guilt. So once in the custody of police, the six were allegedly beaten and deprived of food and sleep and even subjected to a mock execution because the police believed they had their offenders; a theme, sadly, you will see repeated in the cases we will cover in this book.

Four of the six confessed under duress, and in May 1975 all were charged and found guilty of murder and conspiracy to cause explosions. The men later withdrew their coerced confessions, and all six maintained their innocence going forward. In 1991, after significant interest in the case from various media groups questioning the safety of the convictions, the case was referred back to the Court of Appeal. On the basis of police fabricating and suppressing evidence, as well as the unreliability of the confession evidence, the appeal was granted and on 14 March 1991, the Birmingham Six walked free. The Court of Appeal stated that three former detectives had lied to achieve the convictions.

Clearly, this miscarriage of justice was a horrendous experience for the Birmingham Six, who lost more than 16 years of their lives for crimes they did not commit.

Equally appalling, the real mass murderers who were responsible have never been brought to justice. As things stand, the many families impacted by this act of terror will never see anyone prosecuted for these crimes.

In numerous ways, the Birmingham Six case highlights many of the core themes that lead to miscarriages of justice occurring: police going down investigative rabbit holes, unreliable or fabricated evidence, and coerced confessions amongst them.

Sadly, this type of injustice is not limited to Britain, and we will see, as we go through the cases in this book, how reflections are seen within the Australian criminal justice system.

The cases we will look at are not isolated incidents of incompetence or mishandling. They represent systemic failures of our criminal justice system.

We don't seem to be able to learn from our mistakes.

THE FORGOTTEN VICTIMS OF MISCARRIAGES OF JUSTICE

We mostly forget about the wrongly accused and convicted when we think about victims of crime, but in this book I want to highlight some of their stories, because if it happened to them it could happen to anybody. We need to be more open minded when it comes to our blind acceptance that the criminal justice system always gets this right. Because it doesn't.

I wrote about Lindy Chamberlain (now Chamberlain-Creighton) when I published a book on mothers accused of murdering their own children, and Lindy is surely the poster child when we consider people who are wrongly accused. My university students, many in their early 20s, don't know Lindy's name, but they certainly know the story. Lindy and her husband Michael were holidaying at Uluru in August 1980. On the evening of 17 August, Lindy put nine-week-old Azaria to bed in a tent with Azaria's brother Reagan at about 8pm, before Lindy returned to the group of other campers gathered around the barbeques.

A short time later, the group heard a baby's cry from the direction of the tents, and Lindy rushed over to check on her sleeping children. She then uttered what has become an infamous cry: 'My God, the dingo's got my baby!' Azaria vanished that night, and was never seen again. Her body was never recovered.

This was just the start of the horror for the Chamberlains. The police did not believe Lindy and Michael's account, and instead the mother found herself at the centre of one of Australia's most infamous murder trials. She was tried and found guilty of murder on the basis of flawed expert forensic evidence and was sentenced to life imprisonment. Michael was found guilty of being an accessory after the fact. Lindy spent over three years in prison – all for a crime that never happened. She was only released in 1986 when a piece of Azaria's clothing happened to be found near a dingo's lair. All of Lindy and Michael's convictions were subsequently quashed by the Court of Appeal in 1988.

But the nightmare was not over. Speculation still abounded as to what had happened that night, with an inquest held in 1995 recording an open finding. It was not until 2012 – over 30 years after Azaria's death – that Lindy and Michael Chamberlain finally cleared their names of any involvement in the murder of their daughter. At a fourth inquest, the Coroner stated that a dingo took Azaria. An amended death certificate was then issued to reflect the sad truth.

Post-release, Lindy was awarded $1.3 million for wrongful imprisonment, but does this make up for the loss of time with her family whilst incarcerated, the horrendous way she was treated in the media or the subsequent decades of vilification? Of course not. And that was after she suffered the terrible trauma of the loss of a child under violent circumstances.

And still, literally to this day, students will ask me if I think Lindy Chamberlain-Creighton was guilty of intentionally harming Azaria. I rarely get exasperated with students, but this one always pushes my buttons as having personally re-evaluated the evidence in this case, I am totally convinced that Lindy should never have been prosecuted let alone found guilty. So I explain as patiently as I can that 'Lindy no more killed Azaria than I did'. Some of you reading this will still have doubts. Let me put them to rest for you. It was not possible for Lindy to have killed Azaria in the way presented by the Crown in any universe we exist in. Azaria Chamberlain was taken by a dingo. Now can we please move on.

This speaks to the second insult that those who have been wrongfully convicted suffer – the whispers that 'there's no smoke without fire . . .'

Looking at Lindy's case, I asked myself why people find it so hard to believe Lindy was innocent. And I have been left with one lasting impression – Lindy did not behave as mothers 'should' if a child was taken. She was stoical fronting the press. She didn't cry.

In other words, she wasn't 'maternal' enough. She did not behave as society said she should, and therefore she must be guilty. Right? Well, actually, no.

This highlights a core problem in the world of criminal justice – bias. We are all biased, we all judge others and most of the time we don't even know we're doing it.

Ultimately in transient human interactions we are all guilty of judging books by their covers.

We also do that when judging someone's potential guilt.

And when the person doing the judging, applying inherent bias, is a police officer or juror, then serious problems of procedural fairness can arise.

The implications for us all could not be more severe.

Even after a conviction is overturned because it was unjust, as in Lindy's case, and even after the entire legal community acknowledges an error was made (or an entire litany of errors), how do we give these people back what they have lost?

The answer is, we can't.

Years, sometimes decades, in prison, loss of time with loved ones, memories of birthdays, Christmases, weddings they will never have, careers that won't happen, dreams that won't ever come true. And still there will be doubters who think them guilty.

Some of the stories we will discuss here will frighten you, as you will realise how lucky you are if you have never been falsely accused of a crime, because it can be extremely difficult, if not impossible, to demonstrate you weren't involved.

And even without a successful prosecution, even simply an accusation of serious wrongdoing can ruin someone's life. Mud sticks.

For example, in November 2018, Kenan Basic, a 39-year-old father of one, spent two weeks in Silverwater maximum security prison in Sydney, got divorced from his wife and lost his job, all after he simply stopped to help a young woman whose car had broken down. For reasons that have never become clear, after Basic spent two hours working on the car and the woman drove off, unharmed, she reported Basic to the police, accusing him of indecent assault and stalking. The woman retracted all the allegations, but not until May 2019, at which point all charges against Mr Basic were dropped, and clearly not before the incident had already had major repercussions on his entire life.

I can be as guilty as anyone of jumping to conclusions. When I saw this story on the news, I assumed, like most people I would think, that Basic was guilty. I didn't wait until due process had taken place, until I'd heard the evidence in full.

If that case had gone to court, how many of the jurors would already have made up their minds before hearing a word the defence said?

Frightening for anyone who is ever falsely accused.

Other miscarriages of justice occur because of problems with the police investigation itself, commonly confirmation bias and tunnel vision on the part of investigators.

And there is plenty of evidence that confirmation bias (when evidence is interpreted as confirming a pre-existing belief) sends innocent people to prison; just look at the case of the Birmingham Six. In a criminal case, this means that investigators can cherry pick the information they focus on (either consciously or subconsciously), and only give weight to evidence that fits their preconceived notion of what happened. They can then fall into the trap of ignoring other information that doesn't fit their hypothesis, ignoring potential suspects as they've already decided who is guilty, and are only interested in pursuing that one line of inquiry.

When it gets to the point where they are solely focused on building a case against the person/persons they believe to be guilty, to the exclusion of all other possibilities and even exculpatory (from the Latin meaning 'freed from blame') evidence, this is known as tunnel vision.

These problems can be exacerbated following high-profile violent crimes, as the investigators can be placed under serious pressure to solve the case quickly.

I have had personal experience of this when working in forensic investigations. The cases I work on most often comprise of comparisons of images of living people – commonly a suspect in CCTV footage and a person of interest (POI). On initial viewing of the images, understandably the officers will often ask, 'How sure are you they are one and the same person?' They are keen to know the strength of the evidence, but I never, ever comment at that stage. I simply say that, until I have completed my analysis, I can't say. The cart should never go before the horse when it comes to expert opinion.

I also don't want to know any details about the POI's previous convictions for similar offences, or opportunity to have committed this crime.

All of that information is irrelevant to me. I am simply comparing A to B, an image to a POI, and nothing extraneous can be allowed to influence my findings, even subconsciously.

It also doesn't matter to me if I am employed by the prosecution or defence. My report will say the same thing either way. As an expert, my duty, as with all experts, is first and foremost to the court.

That is how I was trained, and I take my responsibility to be objective very seriously, as I've seen too often what can happen if the police and experts allow their opinions to be biased.

I have been criticised for working for the defence, especially in cases of alleged child sexual assault. My answer is always the same: if you, your brother, husband, mother or father, whoever, was accused of a serious offence, wouldn't they deserve the right to be considered innocent until proven otherwise beyond reasonable doubt? And wouldn't you want the experts, charged with providing reports for the investigation, to be objective?

Of course you would. We all would.

An example of a case in which tunnel vision influenced the outcome was the murder of 15-year-old Angela Correa, a high-school student who was raped and murdered in New York in 1989. The police soon focused all of their attention on one of her classmates,

17-year-old Jeffrey Deskovic, having decided he was the culprit. Deskovic was convicted of the crime in 1990, based largely on a false confession he made but later retracted. There was no forensic or other evidence linking him to the crime; in fact, his DNA was excluded as matching DNA retrieved from Angela's body after her murder. His defence counsel made appeals to have post-conviction DNA testing undertaken, which would compare DNA taken from the crime scene to the criminal database, but these appeals were rejected by the District Attorney. Jeffrey served 16 years in prison, and was finally exonerated in 2006 when a new District Attorney approved the DNA comparison, and the actual rapist and murderer was identified, a man already in prison for murder. The offender later confessed and was convicted of killing Angela. Jeffrey has since become an advocate for reform of the criminal justice system, having set up The Jeffrey Deskovic Foundation for Justice, and was awarded $41.6 million in a federal civil suit for wrongful conviction, although he had a pre-trial settlement that limited the payout to $10 million.

But nothing can give back 16 years to a young man falsely accused of the most serious and heinous of crimes. But at least Jeffrey Deskovic found a positive outlet for his experience.

Other miscarriages of justice have very different, heartbreaking endings.

These can result from misleading or inaccurate expert evidence, in terms of both the interpretations and the weight that is attributed to it in court by a jury when deciding someone's guilt beyond reasonable doubt.

An infamous case is that of Sally Clark, a solicitor and daughter of an ex-policeman, who was found guilty of murdering two of her infant sons in the UK in 1996 and 1998. The alternative to Sally having murdered them was that the children died of sudden infant death syndrome (SIDS, also often described as sudden unexpected death in infancy, or SUDI). During the trial in 1999, the prosecution relied heavily on flawed statistical evidence presented by (then) eminent paediatrician Professor Sir Roy Meadow, who simply took the likelihood of one child of a family such as Clark's dying of SIDS as 1:8500 and then multiplied that result by two, reflecting that two babies had died under similar circumstances. This gave a likelihood of both babies dying of SIDS as 1:73 million. He also gave evidence to the jury expressing his personal maxim that 'one sudden infant death in a family is a tragedy, two is suspicious, and three is murder unless proven otherwise'.

This became known as 'Meadow's Law' and was a theory applied during the cases of a number of other British women whose children died. There is, however, no factual or scientific foundation to this statement. A family losing one child to SIDS can actually predispose them to losing other babies, as they may be subject to environmental or genetic risk factors. In fact, the likelihood of Clark losing two babies was more like 1:200.

However, Meadow's flawed evidence was highly compelling to the jury, and Clark was found guilty by a majority jury verdict of 10–2 and given the mandatory life sentence for murder. An appeal against her conviction was unsuccessful in 2000. A second appeal was successful in 2003, and was based on the fact that evidence from the post-mortem of one of the children indicated that he died from natural causes relating to a bacterial infection. As well, defence pathologist, Dr Alan Williams, knew about the exculpatory post-mortem evidence since 1998, but it had not been disclosed to the defence or police. Furthermore, the flaws in Meadow's statistical evidence had been highlighted by the Royal Statistical Society of Britain, which wrote an open letter of complaint to the Lord Chancellor about Meadow's use of statistics in Clark's trial, stating that 'the calculation leading to 1 in 73 million is invalid' and that there was no statistical basis for this figure.

Sally Clark was released in January 2003, but the fact that she had been a solicitor and was the daughter of an ex-policeman, as well as her status as a child-killer, meant she had suffered more than most in prison, having been targeted by other inmates. She struggled to readjust on release, even though her husband and family had always stood by her and publicly protested her innocence. Sally was unable to recover from the effects of her prosecution and incarceration. She was diagnosed with serious resultant psychiatric problems, as well as alcohol dependency, and died as a result of acute alcohol intoxication in 2007. A tragic end to an awful situation that should not have happened.

Sir Roy Meadow was struck off the register by the General Medical Council in 2005 for serious professional misconduct, although he was reinstated following appeal in 2006. Dr Alan Williams also suffered significant, and in my view justified, professional criticism and was suspended from performing Home Office post-mortems for 18 months. The consequences for Meadow and Williams were far less than for the Clark family.

The repercussions of Meadow's flawed expert evidence went further. Following Clark's release in January 2003, the Attorney General ordered a review of all similar cases; those involving mothers accused of murdering their own children in which Meadow had given expert testimony. As a result, Angela Cannings (found guilty of murdering her two sons in 2002) and Donna Anthony (convicted of murdering her two babies in 1998) had their convictions quashed and were released from prison, and Trupti Patel was acquitted of killing her three children in June 2003. By this time Donna had spent over six years in prison and Angela more than a year. Although very distressing, Trupti was lucky in that by the time her case was heard in court, Meadow had been largely discredited, so she was not subject to the same bias as Cannings and Anthony.

THE CASES WE WILL LOOK AT

As we will see, we are not immune; miscarriages of justice do happen in Australia, too. For example, in October 2019, former Treasury official David Eastman was awarded $7 million in compensation for his wrongful conviction for the murder of Canberra's police chief, Colin Winchester, who was shot at close range as he got out of his car in January 1989. Eastman became a suspect in the shooting as he had met Winchester in an effort to avoid an assault charge. David was found guilty of the murder and sentenced to life. He spent 19 years in prison, until his conviction was finally quashed and a retrial ordered after a judicial inquiry found that there had been a miscarriage of justice. The jury in a second trial in 2018 found Eastman not guilty of Winchester's murder. How did this happen? No murder weapon was ever recovered, and the only direct link between Eastman and the crime scene, identified by forensic expert Robert Barnes of the Victorian State Forensic Science Laboratory, was gunshot residue from David's car that matched the residue from the scene. However, Barnes' comparative methods and his record-keeping were called into question at the inquiry into Eastman's conviction. Worse, the prosecution had seen red flags regarding Barnes' work, and had asked a number of international experts to review his work in relation to the Eastman case. These experts also identified issues with Barnes' scientific method and record-keeping, which undermined the reliability of his evidence as an expert witness, yet the prosecution did not disclose many of these issues to the defence. The inquiry found this non-disclosure also had severe implications on the case, as had the defence known, they could have mounted a robust – and likely successful – challenge to the only forensic evidence against the accused.

So serious were the concerns over Barnes' work that the ACT Supreme Court described his evidence as 'completely untrustworthy, and ought not to [have been] allowed to enter into the reasons for any verdict of guilty'. Yet another man spent years in prison, partly on the basis of misleading expert testimony and procedural short-comings, the actual killer escaped justice, and the Winchester family is left without the answers and justice it deserves.

The first possible wrongful conviction we will review in detail is the murder of Celia Douty in 1983, and subsequent conviction of Wayne Butler. I became good friends with a DNA expert, Professor Barry Boettcher, who told me about this case as he has serious doubts as to the reliability of the evidence used to convict Butler. Did the original experts that assessed the DNA between the murder scene and Butler make an error? I don't know, and I am not convinced either way as to Butler's guilt. But I am concerned that one type of evidence (DNA) was used to convict a man of murder, with only vague circumstantial evidence to support the prosecution's case. No forensic technique is infallible, even a DNA match.

The second case reflects a common thread you will, unfortunately, quickly come to recognise as a core reason for wrongful convictions: coerced confessions as a result of police suffering tunnel vision. In 1983 Kelvin Condren, a young Indigenous man, was charged with the murder of his girlfriend, Patricia Carlton. The victim had been brutally murdered, but Kelvin had a water-tight alibi: he was in police custody at the time of Patricia's death. Nonetheless, he confessed to the crime, after being threatened by police during interview. He later retracted his confession. One month after his arrest and before his trial, a violent offender confessed to Patricia's murder, but the prosecution persevered with their case and convinced the jury of Kelvin's guilt. He was found guilty and sentenced to life in prison. This error did not come to light until a journalist started asking questions and found the truth. Kelvin was Aboriginal, unemployed, and an easy target for police. More than just demonstrating that police can go down investigative rabbit holes, Kelvin's conviction raises serious issues of inequality in the meting out of justice, as those from vulnerable backgrounds are more likely to suffer wrongful convictions.

Chapter three also looks at a case where the police failed to consider all of the evidence and coerced a confession, which led to a vulnerable man diagnosed with bipolar disorder, Andrew Mallard, being convicted of the murder of Pamela Lawrence. Andrew was just in the wrong place at the wrong time. Again a journalist raised doubts over the conviction and, with the help of a politician, Andrew's conviction was eventually overturned. It later transpired that officers investigating Pamela's murder withheld evidence from the defence, in direct violation of legal protocol. These officers were later found guilty of misconduct. Forensic evidence at the murder scene eventually led the police to the likely culprit, but sadly not before he had brutally murdered another woman. The cost of this wrongful conviction was high indeed.

Henry Keogh and the death of his fiancée, Anna-Jane Cheney, are the subject of chapter four. Henry was convicted of Anna-Jane's murder on the basis of flawed forensic evidence by forensic pathologist Dr Colin Manock. Across his career Manock undertook more than 10,000 post-mortems and was a very senior forensic pathologist in South Australia, however, he had an extensive history of reaching erroneous conclusions, possibly as a result of the fact that he had absolutely no qualifications in forensic pathology. Anna-Jane's death was a tragic accidental drowning and because of Manock, Henry spent almost 20 years in prison. Worse, Manock gave expert evidence in dozens of other cases, including cases of child deaths, some of which in my opinion may have resulted in murderers going free. This case shows the damage that can be done by one renegade 'expert'.

In chapter five we review the death of Albert Snowball, a young man who fell to his death in 2005. Young boxer Khalid Baker was found guilty of his murder, even though numerous witnesses claim he was nowhere near the deceased at the time of his fall. More impactful, Khalid's best friend, LM, openly admitted many times that he was the last one to touch Albert, and if anyone were responsible for his death it was him, not Khalid. But the jury were convinced of Khalid's guilt, and he spent 13 years in prison. He maintains his innocence to this day, supported by LM, and is still fighting to clear his name as, although he is now on parole, he remains, in the eyes of the law, a convicted murderer. This case raises questions of racial bias, another worrying staple of miscarriages of justice.

No book about miscarriages of justice in Australia could ignore the case of 'Lawyer X', or Nicola Gobbo, as we now know her. Gobbo was a defence barrister who played both sides of the line, informing on her high-profile clients to Victoria Police. This went on for years, and a significant number of cases were successfully prosecuted, partly on the basis of Gobbo's contributions. But Gobbo's actions were in direct violation of her duties to her clients leading to a case of legal corruption like Australia has never seen before. It all became a very public mess in 2019, when Victoria Police and Gobbo lost their long legal battles to keep her name a secret. Dozens of cases have been affected, and some very dangerous people will be able to contest the legitimacy of their prosecutions, claiming (perhaps correctly) that Gobbo's involvement in their cases has led to miscarriages of justice. The fallout from this is going to be felt for years, and this case is an interesting example when assessing who we class as 'victims' of potential injustice.

So, together, the cases cover factual problems (such as evidence another person was involved or the accused simply could not have committed the crime as described), expert witnesses making errors in evidence collection, processing or interpretation, as well as procedural problems on the part of the police or courts, as all of these can lead to miscarriages of justice. Issues relating to eyewitnesses' identifications will also be discussed, as what people see and remember is not as clear cut as you might imagine.

Some of the cases are recognised formally as miscarriages of justice, some as wrongful convictions. In other cases an alleged criminal may still be in prison, yet there are question marks over the reliability of their conviction – I have included them, not because I am saying they are necessarily innocent, but rather that the evidence may not stack up to support a conclusion of guilty beyond reasonable doubt.

Regardless of the cause, there is always very significant trauma caused by miscarriages of justice, for the wrongly accused, their family and friends, and the community as a whole.

And let's not forget, when a wrongful conviction is overturned, and an innocent person is released, if a murder or other serious crime has taken place, this then re-traumatises the victim and their family, as they face the reality that the person who harmed them is potentially still out there.

One thing that will become very obvious as we look at the cases I have selected is that miscarriages of justice happen much more frequently to people who are already marginalised or disadvantaged in our society. Whether as a result of race, sex, disability, or low educational status, those who experience discrimination more broadly are likely to experience bias in the justice system at all stages.

Again and again, we will see vulnerable people targeted, without the resources or knowledge of the system to fight. It is a David and Goliath battle and most of the time they lose.

I trained as a forensic scientist to help victims of crime, working with the police to bring those responsible to justice or the defence to provide expert evidence for trial to help ensure only the guilty go to prison. So I have a very personal interest in the workings – and failings – of our criminal justice system. As an observer of when it has gone horribly wrong, as well as an active participant, I also have a stake in trying to improve the system.

To do my job, I need to think that most of the time we get it right. And I believe we do.

However, as you will see, sometimes we fail spectacularly. And that frightens me.

In the words of Mark Leveson, father of Matthew Leveson, who died under mysterious circumstances in 2007, 'It's not a justice system. It's just a system.'

Sadly, this is very true. For every case I have included there are 100 others I could have chosen, which would have highlighted the same failings and errors that led to an innocent person going to prison.

But the individual stories are important, as they allow us to emotionally engage with those who have suffered, to give real-world context to the problems we'll discuss, and help us realise that people being falsely accused and prosecuted for crimes is a problem that can and does affect us all.

ONE

WAYNE BUTLER:
DID HE MURDER CELIA DOUTY?
(1983)

'DNA evidence cannot . . . prove of itself that someone is
guilty beyond reasonable doubt.'

The University of New South Wales Council for Civil Liberties

Brampton Island is paradise. A small 460-hectare island lying at
the southern end of the world-famous Whitsunday Passage and
within the Great Barrier Reef World Heritage Area. Tourists are
drawn to its resort to enjoy year-round tropical temperatures,
isolated beaches, kilometres of walking tracks that take in sparkling
azure waters, breathtaking rainforests, lush coastal mangroves, and
of course coral reefs, home to stunning marine life.

But this haven of relaxation was rocked in September 1983
when 40-year-old resort worker Celia 'Tasha' Douty was brutally
murdered whilst sunbathing on one of the island's many sandy and
secluded beaches.

The case remained unsolved until 2001, when Wayne Butler,
a Sydney-based business manager, was accused and found guilty

of Celia's murder. This case stands out because it was the first in Australia to be solved on the basis of DNA evidence, recovered from items found at the murder scene allegedly linking Butler to the crime.

However, doubts have been raised over the years, notably again in 2019 when a high-profile and well-respected DNA expert, Professor Barry Boettcher, cast serious doubt on whether the DNA at the scene was in fact the accused's. I became interested in this case after meeting Barry and hearing his concerns. We spent many hours going over the evidence, and debating the strengths of the DNA evidence. I still don't know if I think Butler killed Celia, but I am concerned that just one type of evidence was used to convict a man of murder, and it certainly warranted a closer look.

Over a quarter of a century after Celia's murder, it looked like the case was about to blow open again, as perhaps an innocent man had been imprisoned for her brutal murder.

THE CASE

Celia Douty was lucky enough to have landed a summer job working at the beautiful tourist resort on Brampton Island, off the coast of Queensland. It was a world away from the one she'd known in Warwickshire, England, before she emigrated to Australia to enjoy her new life in the sun. She loved Brampton Island, writing to her family that she wanted to stay forever in paradise.

Sadly, she would get her wish.

On 31 August 1983, she took a short ferry trip to the town of Mackay on the mainland for a dentist appointment, and spent the night there, before returning to Brampton on the morning of 1 September by ferry.

Celia went straight to her accommodation to drop off some items she had purchased in Mackay, before heading to secluded

Dinghy Bay, known for nude sunbathing, taking with her a brand new red beach towel she had also just bought.

She got to the beach around 10:40am, but was only there a short time, as a pilot who had flown directly over the bay said she was not there at 11am. Her killer had moved quickly.

Celia was due to return to work at the resort on 2 September, but she didn't show. This wasn't like her, and her colleagues became concerned enough that they contacted the police and a search quickly ensued. Although the exploration of the island was complicated by the fact it is covered in mangroves and many parts are only accessible on foot, the island is so small that it did not take long to find Celia's naked body at the bay, hidden in the scrub and covered by her red beach towel.

Blood spatter evidence suggested she had been killed near the water. There was a large pool of blood a short distance from where her body was located. Around this main pool of blood was radiating spatter of up to about 2 metres, and up to 60 centimetres above ground level, splashing nearby vegetation. That the spatter pattern was so widespread indicates the blows that killed Celia were of considerable force.

Celia died of blunt force trauma to the head, having been hit repeatedly with a large rock. Celia's body was covered with vegetation and soil, and was also heavily bloodstained, particularly around her head and neck, as well as her shoulders and chest. The blood patterning indicated that Celia had died whilst lying on her back, and that her head had been struck whilst it was close to the ground.

As Celia was discovered away from the main area of blood pooling, this indicates she was moved to the position she was found in after she had been killed.

EXPERT INSERT: BLOOD SPATTER

Bloodstain pattern analysis, or BPA, can provide useful invest-igative information in criminal cases, and it helps experts recreate the events that caused the bloodshed. This is possible as blood behaves in predictable ways, according to certain principles. Individual blood drops, as well as the patterns they form, are both useful.

Blood stains at scenes, or on physical evidence recovered from a crime scene (such as clothing an offender or victim may have been wearing during the incident), can help the expert determine a number of key factors that relate to how the patterns were created, including:

- The location and position of the victim when injuries were caused (sitting, standing etc.)
- The relative position of the offender to the victim
- The origin(s) of the blood
- The weapon that likely caused the injury (for example, something sharp such as a knife, or a blunt item such as a stone, as these would create different spatter patterns)
- The direction from which the victim was wounded, and the number of contacts (if any, for example, in a shooting, the gun may not come in direct contact with the victim, but the bullet trajectory could be tracked using BPA)
- The sequence of events that created the spatter patterns
- How many potential offenders were present, and which may have caused the injuries
- What level of force is likely to have been employed
- The movement of the victim(s), persons of interest, or relevant objects at the scene, both during and after the bloodshed

Different types of patterns are formed by different actions. 'Drip stain' occurs as a result of a falling drop that formed due to gravity. For example, blood drops falling off the end of a knife held at height. This can extend into a 'drip-trail' if there is movement between two points. 'Cast-off' patterns arise when blood drops are released due to an object's motion, for example a hammer hitting a person and causing blood to be transferred to the weapon, and being pulled back for a second blow. 'Impact patterns' occur when an object strikes liquid blood, such as the pattern created on a person's shoe if they walked through a pool of wet blood.

To provide information on these factors, experts assess the size and shape of the blood spatter, as well as the location and distribution. Bloodstain pattern analysis is highly scientific and draws on various principles: biological, in that the behaviour of blood is evaluated; physics, when interpreting the velocity, cohesion and capillary action (which affect the shape of the blood as it moves as a result of the fact that the tension on the surface of the blood drop binds the molecules together); and mathematics, in that factors such as distance from the source and geometry are measured.

Just as important as determining what happened is establishing what did not happen. In this way BPA can help corroborate or refute witness statements.

A case that centred on BPA and its value in determining the aetiology of an event is the 1994 murder of 64-year-old Las Vegas real estate magnate Ronald Rudin. The victim's charred remains were found at a lake in 1995, with three bullet holes in his skull. Ronald's remains were identified via dental records.

Suspicion soon fell on his wife Margaret, as she behaved suspiciously when the police delivered the death notification. They also learnt she had accused Ronald (her fifth husband) of having affairs, and he had specifically requested in his will that additional investigation take place should he die a violent and unnatural death. Prosecutors also learnt that Margaret was worried Ronald was going to divorce her, and she would lose millions of dollars in inheritance.

Meanwhile, the police had searched the family home and found a .22 gun missing from the collection. As well, brownish-red spots were located on the bedroom ceiling. Hemastix was used to test the stains; it was confirmed they were blood and showed a massive area of blood spatter.

Complicating the picture was the fact that 10 years previously, Ronald's first wife, Peggy Rudin, committed suicide in the same room by shooting herself in the head. The question then arose – was the blood patterning new and did it have anything to do with Ronald's death, or was it from Peggy's suicide?

By measuring the length and width of each stain, as well as using lasers to determine the origin of each spot of blood, crime scene investigators were able to use trigonometry to determine the angle of impact and path of each spot. Spatter trajectories and patterns illustrated that there were two different points of origin. Therefore, two different deaths, or at least traumatic events, had occurred in that room.

The police also searched Lake Mead, where Ronald's body had been found, and discovered the missing .22 gun. This was the last piece of evidence they needed to arrest Margaret. After she became a suspect, Margaret went on the run, using a false name and travelling to Mexico and back to the US, hiding in Arizona and Massachusetts, where she was arrested for her husband's murder in 1999 after someone recognised her from the TV program *America's Most Wanted*. She was found guilty and sentenced to 20 years in prison.

Without BPA it might not have been possible to determine what had occurred at the crime scene, and therefore who was responsible for Ronald's murder.

Tim Doran, Assistant Chief of Police in Colorado and a retired Federal Bureau of Investigation Special Agent

Celia's personal possessions, including her bag and clothes, had been taken by her attacker and have never been located.

DNA profiling would not be used in a forensic investigation until 1986, so prior to this, offenders were far more brazen in the evidence they left at crime scenes; they simply were not aware of the new techniques that could, or would in the future, be used to trace them.

There was both blood and semen found on the red beach towel, which was also covered with vegetation and sand. The semen was found in six different places, widely spaced apart; five were found on the upper-most surface, and the sixth on the surface that was in contact with the body. The semen did not soak through, and, with one exception (labelled 'semen stain 3'), were not heavy – they likely represented single drops.

The one large area looked like a 'spread' of semen across the surface of the towel, and comprised of five stains. The pattern indicated that the offender's penis was above the towel when it ejaculated the semen onto it.

There was no semen found within Celia's vagina or mixed with the blood samples recovered from the towel.

The large area of blood at one end of the towel belonged to the deceased, and, we have to assume, the semen to her killer, meaning the killer's DNA would be available for comparison to a potential perpetrator when one was identified.

Scientists from Queensland's Forensic and Scientific Services mortuary, commonly known as the John Tonge Centre (JTC), the state's major DNA testing laboratory, took possession of the bloody beach towel and conducted tests on it. There was clearly a large area of blood, and acid phosphate testing (an enzyme found in semen, mainly in early portions of ejaculate) on six pieces of towel indicated the presence of the semen. The location and patterning of the stains indicated that they had been created through masturbation, as opposed to intercourse, as there was no vaginal material from Celia intermixed in any of the samples. This confirmed the post-mortem results, as there was no evidence of recent sexual activity, including sexual assault.

Also found in the vicinity of Celia's body, near the main pool of blood, was a pair of blue thongs which had dried blood on the soles as well as on the upper surfaces. A yellow and red 'Makita' cap was also recovered.

The police worked hard to find Celia's attacker, interviewing 300 guests and visitors on the island, and the Queensland Government offered a $30,000 reward for information leading to the arrest and conviction of the person responsible for her murder, but no one claimed it and no witnesses to the murder were identified.

In addition, they offered immunity to any person involved in the attack who came forward with information first, as long as they weren't the person who actually killed her.

The police were keen to solve this case quickly, not only because the crime was particularly brutal, but also because of the political pressure to see someone brought to justice. This was a nightmare for Queensland's tourism industry, as the Whitsunday Island group was a tourist mecca. A violent murder on one of the group's most popular islands could impact Queensland's economy for years to come.

But they had few clues, and because of the isolated location of the crime, together with the transitory nature of the population – holiday-makers and day-trippers – their job was made even harder.

But they did have one lead. This related to a man and woman, seen in the area at the time, having visited Brampton as day-trippers on the ferry. They were described on the reward poster:

A male person about 38 years of age, medium height, athletic looking and well built, dark hair possibly going grey. The woman is described as being mid to late thirties, very small build, bleached blonde shoulder length hair. She is extremely well sun-tanned, very noticeable and easily identified.

The police were keen to speak to this couple, who had been witnessed having a heated argument on the ferry on the way back to Mackay from Brampton on the afternoon of 1 September. Witnesses described the content of the argument focusing on the woman being angry that the man had left her alone for around four hours, telling her he was going for a jog and walk along the trails that criss-cross the island.

For years the identity of the man and woman would remain a mystery.

THE EVIDENCE

The case went cold for almost five years. Then a breakthrough.

In 1988, the police were contacted by a man who said he believed he knew the couple that were arguing on the Brampton

Island ferry; he identified his brother, Wayne Butler, as the man they were looking for, and Wayne's wife, Vija Samite Duffy, as the blonde woman.

Why Wayne's brother would come forward five years after the murder is unclear, but perhaps he believed his brother and his wife might have vital evidence that could solve the crime, without believing Wayne was the guilty party.

When the police spoke to Wayne he confirmed that he had gone for jog and walk around the island on the morning Celia was killed, whilst Vija had stayed at the resort sunbathing. They were the couple overheard arguing on the ferry back to the mainland on the afternoon of 1 September, as Vija had been annoyed that Butler had left her alone for so long, around four hours, to which Wayne responded that he had not realised that the island was so big.

He had been seen by witnesses, and was wearing running shoes, not blue thongs.

Other witnesses told police, however, that Celia had been on the ferry back to Brampton Island on the morning of 1 September (the same ferry as Butler and Duffy), with the brand new beach towel she had purchased in Mackay. Several people reported overhearing her telling her friends that she planned to sunbathe at Dinghy Bay when she got back.

The inference the police reached was that Butler had overheard this conversation, and that he had made an excuse to get away from his wife for a few hours with the express intention of seeking Celia out. There is no evidence for this, only the police hypothesis, as they had to find a link between Wayne and Celia, to fit in with what another witness told them – that Butler had stopped them to ask for directions to Dinghy Bay.

The police now had Wayne in their sights. They had means and opportunity, and he was arrested on 28 September 1988. The police searched his home but nothing of relevance was found. Wayne gave a voluntary sample of blood and saliva on 29 September for comparative purposes, after which he was released.

But the capacity to identify perpetrators via DNA at the time of Celia's murder was still limited to determining the blood group of the offender, rather than being able to create a DNA profile as we could do today.

Blood group (ABO) testing was conducted on the six separate sections of towel that had contained semen on three different occasions. Generally, the tests failed to produce a result, however 'semen stain 3' was tested twice on 16 September 1983 and on 23 January 1984. This sample returned results indicating the donor of the sperm was 'O' blood group. 'Semen stain 5' also gave a weak result of the donor being O group, when tested on 4 April 1984. These variations in results are to be expected, as different portions of the ejaculate comprise of different compositions of material, some of which will respond to acid phosphate more strongly than others.

The most common blood group in Australia is O positive, with around 38 per cent of the population sharing this blood group, and another seven per cent are O negative – meaning blood group O encompasses around 45 per cent of the population. Blood group B (combined positive and negative) only makes up about 10 per cent of all Australians, making it one of the least common.

Wayne's blood was then tested. To undertake this comparison, some of Wayne's blood was used to saturate a white cloth that was then dried. This cloth then became part of the investigation, case number 14467, and the piece from which DNA was extracted was given the number 14467–9. In turn, the item for DNA extraction, and the DNA derived from it, was given the tracking number '12151'.

The comparison came back as a non-match; Butler was found to have blood group B.

As it is generally impossible for blood types to change (except under exceptional circumstances, such as someone having received a bone marrow transplant), this precluded Butler from being the donor of the semen found on the beach towel.

Worryingly, although the white cloth containing Wayne's blood was stored, his biological samples (blood and saliva) were then discarded and no documentation was completed for them. And this at a facility that specialises in forensic DNA work.

Butler was arrested, but without enough evidence and with the negative blood group match, the charges against him were dropped and he was released. However, Wayne remained the police's main suspect, but without more evidence to go on there was nothing they could do, and again the case went cold.

An inquest into Celia's murder held in 1989 and 1990 was inconclusive, and regardless of the non-matching blood group tests, Butler remained a person of interest (POI) to police.

And in time, Wayne's family would turn on him again. In 1997, his now ex-wife, Vija, went to police, telling them that she believed her husband was guilty of Celia's murder. She said that she couldn't tell them whilst they were still married, as she had been afraid of Butler. But, now they were divorced, she wanted to tell the truth.

This is not an uncommon phenomenon. Loyalties change, and as time passes and relationships break down, people sometimes go to the police with information on cold cases. This can be as a result of genuine anxiety to relieve themselves of the burden of knowing or suspecting someone has committed a crime, because the fear of retribution has diminished, or through a desire for personal revenge for an actual or perceived wrong. The police then have to make value judgments as to the motivation of the person providing the intelligence, as that will impact the weight that should be attributed to it.

Vexatious stories waste police resources, but genuine intelligence can break cold cases open.

And time was now on the police's side, in that DNA technology had advanced in the intervening 14 years since Celia's death. Even though Butler's blood group had been found to be a non-match to the killer's, as blood grouping was now considered to have been superseded by DNA profiling (which allows a one-to-one match), the ABO technique was discounted as excluding Butler as a suspect.

EXPERT INSERT: DNA PROFILING

Deoxyribonucleic acid (DNA) is a chemical substance present in the nucleus of cells, and is often referred to as our genetic blueprint. The genetic information coded for by DNA is inherited from one generation to the next and it contains all of the instructions necessary for life. The basic unit of DNA is a nucleotide and it is comprised of three parts: 1) a base, 2) a sugar molecule, and 3) a phosphate group. The bases join together to form base pairs, and to each of these is attached a sugar molecule and a phosphate group. These nucleotides are arranged into two long strands that form the famous DNA double helix, which looks similar to a ladder; with the base pairs forming the rungs, and the phosphate and sugar backbone forming the side rails.

Human DNA is made up of approximately 3 billion bases, and in general, all of the cells of the human body share the same DNA. The four different bases are adenine (A), guanine (G), cytosine (C), and thymine (T); and it is the order of these bases that differs between humans (and all other living things). Over 99 per cent of human DNA is the same, meaning that almost all DNA bases occur in the same order in everybody. It is the differences in the order of the remaining one per cent of bases that make each of us (except identical twins) genetically unique.

Since the invention of DNA fingerprinting by British scientist Alec Jeffreys and the polymerase chain reaction (PCR) by American scientist Kary Mullis in the mid-1980s, modern DNA profiling techniques have evolved to a point where we are able to rapidly extract and profile DNA from a range of biological samples recovered from a crime scene (commonly blood, semen, saliva, tissue, bone, nail, or hair). For trace or compromised samples, the DNA is often limited in quantity and/or quality, but due to improvements in the sensitivity of the technology, a DNA profile is still often obtainable.

Once a DNA profile is obtained, a comparison can then be performed between the evidence sample and a person of interest (POI) such as a victim, suspect, or relative. Alternatively, a DNA database can be searched to see if it can be matched to a known person. Even if no match is found, DNA profiling can link crime scenes (for example, DNA recovered from the offender's semen in one sexual assault case may link to similar sexual assault cases), or pieces of evidence to a crime scene (for example, DNA recovered on a knife abandoned after a stabbing may link to a gun from a shooting murder).

This is possible because a person's DNA profile consists of a set of repeating regions of DNA known as short tandem repeats (STRs), and the variation in the patterns of these STR markers allows individuals to be distinguished from each other. Different countries have different requirements as to how many STR markers are routinely profiled and/or uploaded to the DNA database for forensic casework; currently in the UK it is 16, in Europe it is at least 12, and in the US and Australia it is 20. In addition, a sex marker is also tested to determine if the sample donor is male or female.

DNA profiling is considered a reliable and robust method under standard conditions, in terms of being able to identify a match between an evidence sample and a POI. When no match is found, a POI can be excluded as the source of the evidence. If a match occurs, the POI is included as a potential source of the evidence. In this case, a match statistic is provided to indicate the strength (or weight) of this match (as opposed to matching by chance). Using the most discriminatory DNA test available today, it is estimated that only one person in about every 1 nonillion (1 x 1030) will have a particular STR profile. When you consider that the world's population is approximately 7.8 billion (7.8 x 109) people in 2020, the probability of two unrelated people sharing the same DNA profile is very small.

A new DNA tool being used to solve crimes is familial DNA searching. When a DNA database search does not result in any direct matches, a familial search of the DNA database could identify biological relatives (parents, children, or siblings) of the sample donor. This technique is based on relatives sharing similar and predictable patterns in their DNA profiles. For example, a parent would be expected to share half of their STR markers with their child because a person's DNA is inherited equally from their mother and father. If a potential POI were identified, directly comparing their DNA profile with that of the evidence sample would then confirm or refute the hypothesis that they are the sample donor.

In 2017, serial rapist Patrick Perkins was sentenced to 12 years' jail after this technology was used to link him to two sexual assaults in North Adelaide in 2012. The familial search identified a biological son of Perkins on the South Australian DNA Database, and a DNA sample subsequently collected from him covertly matched the DNA profile recovered from the evidence samples.

One of the other areas where DNA advances have had the most significant impact is for cold cases. In 2019, Terry Hickson was found guilty of stabbing 72-year-old Charles Skarratt to death in his garage in 1989. Skarratt was a wealthy bookmaker and Hickson was attempting to rob him of his winnings after he returned home from the Dapto greyhound races. Blood evidence collected from the victim's sock and car boot at the scene was recently examined using STR profiling methods and compared to a reference DNA sample obtained from Hickson, resulting in a DNA match. If the evidence had not been successfully analysed three decades later using modern DNA technology, Hickson would not have been linked to this case and the case would have remained unsolved.

Associate Professor Jodie Ward, Forensic DNA Identification Specialist at NSW Health Pathology and Director of the Australian Facility for Taphonomic Experimental Research at University of Technology Sydney

In 1997, this advanced DNA technology, which comprised DNA amplification (small sections of DNA can be replicated millions of times, providing more DNA for analysis), was used to undertake a one-to-one comparison between DNA extracted from the semen found on the towel against Butler's DNA profile, as taken from the white cloth that was still being stored at the JTC. This comprised 14 samples taken from around the semen stains, including six areas that were cut out and stored in tubes.

Slides were then produced to allow the samples to be assessed for the presence of sperm, and the one that had the greatest number of sperm present was chosen for DNA extraction. This sample had already been cut out of the towel, and had been given the reference number '12150'.

The extracted DNA from 12150 was then compared to Butler's sample (reference 12151). Experts from the centre were of the opinion that the DNA profiles were a match – the police concluded they had their killer.

Butler was again arrested for Celia's murder on the basis of this new DNA evidence. He maintained his innocence.

His trial for murder commenced in January 2001. The Crown's case was founded on the fact that Butler had the opportunity to kill Celia owing to the fact he left his wife for four hours on the day Celia was murdered, and the 'match' between the semen stains and Butler's DNA sample. The evidence was compelling – the jury being told the likelihood of the DNA profile matching anyone else's was 43 trillion to one. That is a powerful statistic.

Wayne maintained he was not present when Celia died, and his defence rested on the claim that the DNA evidence was unreliable.

Butler did not give evidence in his defence. His ex-wife Vija did, however, speaking to the gap when her husband disappeared, but stating that this was not unusual for him, and adding that when he returned he showed no signs of distress or anxiety, and that she saw no evidence of blood either on Wayne or his clothes. This, even though she had gone to the police and told them she believed her ex-husband was guilty of Celia's murder.

Two DNA experts gave evidence for the Crown. The first was international DNA expert Dr Bruce Budowle, and the second was Mr Leo Freney, Supervising Forensic Scientist in the Forensic Biology Section at the John Tonge Centre, who oversaw the testing of the semen undertaken in 1997.

Butler had access to Dr Kary Mullis, a Nobel Prize–winning American biochemist and world leader in DNA techniques, both as an adviser and as an expert witness in his defence, but Mullis was not called at trial.

Dr Budowle gave evidence, stating that partial degradation would not prevent good results from being obtained. He also noted that 14 years is not a long time for viable DNA to remain, as certainly full profiles have been obtained from samples that are decades old.

The Crown then came to address the fact that the original ABO test undertaken in 1983 appeared to exonerate the accused, and yet the DNA comparison in 1997 between the semen on the towel and Butler's DNA matched.

To explain this discrepancy, it was suggested that the ABO test was erroneous, in that the test may have been affected by bacteria or moisture, or a number of other factors. Further, Celia was blood group O, so the result actually reflected her blood group and not the offender's. This was further supported by the fact that the one test that returned a result was conducted on the part of the towel where the sperm count was the weakest.

The question over the seemingly contradicting results of the ABO and the one-to-one DNA comparison was apparently settled. As a result, the jury clearly believed the DNA evidence over the blood grouping, as after only 90 minutes' deliberation, they found Butler guilty of Celia's murder.

In sentencing, Supreme Court Justice John Helman told Butler, 'For this savage crime you will spend the rest of your days in captivity . . . Parole will always be out of the question.'

This was a landmark case, and a famous conviction – both for the Queensland Police Service as well as for Australia more generally, as this was the first conviction in Australia achieved on the basis of DNA profiling.

It was therefore seen as a flagship case for the new DNA technology.

The Douty family was, understandably, relieved, with Sean, Celia's son, stating after the trial concluded that, 'For my family, my brother and myself, now we can have some closure of the hell that we have endured.'

But for the family it wasn't over, as the wheels of the criminal justice system were going to continue to turn in this case.

In 2001 Butler appealed his conviction on the grounds that it was 'unsafe and unsatisfactory' due to the DNA evidence – the only evidence against him – being unreliable because contamination or degradation may have occurred to the original DNA sample in the intervening 14 years since the murder. Mr Callaghan, acting for Butler, stated that over those 14 years there had been no satisfactory evidence of the condition in which it had been stored, and that various extraneous factors – such as heat or light, or chemicals – could have affected the DNA results and made them unreliable. To further explain how, he suggested that the DNA which the scientists said was taken from the towel was actually DNA taken from one of Wayne's own donated biological samples (either the blood or saliva) in error, and that there was a reasonable hypothesis that Butler was innocent and the verdict unsafe.

The court accepted that there were no records covering the entire 14 years since the original samples were taken, but did not accept that there was any evidence to suggest the conditions required for the DNA to have degraded or become contaminated were present.

The appeal judges stated that there 'was DNA evidence that it was his semen that was found on the red towel'.

However, the judgment also recorded that whilst it was accepted that the DNA profiling gave a more reliable result than ABO testing, this was 'not sufficient to explain why the ABO test was wrong'.

Therefore, on the basis of the evidence given by Budowle and Freney, the appeal was dismissed.

But Butler and his legal team weren't giving up, and a plea was lodged with the then Governor of Queensland, Quentin Bryce, based on new evidence not available at the time of the original trial.

On 29 September 2005, Butler's second appeal opened, but due to the defence requesting additional testing on the DNA of sperm on the slides prepared at JTC in 1997, it was adjourned. These new tests were to be performed by Professor Ian Findlay at Gribble's Molecular Science Pty Ltd, Brisbane. Ultimately, Professor Findlay considered the results of the tests to be inconclusive, as meaningful conclusions could not be drawn from the insufficient results obtained from the badly degraded DNA extracted from the sperm on the slides.

In February 2006, two samples of the red towel (referenced as samples 14467–7–1 and 14467–6–1–1) were sent from the John Tonge Centre to Robert Goetz at the Division of Analytical Laboratories, Lidcombe, NSW. Only sample 14467–7–1 was tested. Sperm was found, the DNA from which matched Butler's DNA profile.

I have discussed this result with Professor Boettcher, as it would appear from these independent tests that Butler was indeed the donor of the sperm on the red beach towel. However, Barry does not agree. After reviewing all of the documents that detail all tests on the various exhibits in this case, he concluded that the records relating to the original samples and their handling was inconsistent with the labelling.

Consequently, Boettcher states that the origin of the samples tested at the Division of Analytical Laboratories cannot be established to the required legal standard to be considered reliable.

The appeal was finally heard after all of the additional tests had been conducted, and was held from 23 to 25 March 2009. This was possible after Butler's legal team contacted the Attorney General of Queensland seeking a pardon or retrial on the grounds that the DNA evidence used to convict him was unreliable, as it was, according to Butler, corrupted at the John Tonge Centre. The Attorney General referred Butler's petition for a pardon to the Supreme Court of Queensland, Court of Appeal, as a result of the new DNA evidence available that was not presented to the court during the original trial.

The new appeal court heard evidence from numerous witnesses, not least of whom was Professor Barry Boettcher.

Boettcher, a recognised expert in blood group compounds in body secretions, including semen, tested a sample of Butler's semen in 2012, 17 days after it was produced – comparable with the elapse of time before the first blood grouping tests on semen stains on the red towel that covered Douty's body. He found that Butler's semen had a 'group B' to 'group O' ratio of 8:1 – an average ratio for a group B male. He commented that tests on a stain of Butler's semen would be expected to show both 'B' and 'O' activity. On this basis, he considered that the semen stains on the red towel, where only 'O' activity was detected, could not have originated from Butler.

Boettcher's knowledge of blood group compounds in semen from group B males, before he had conducted any tests on Butler's semen, led him to look for an error in the DNA testing.

Boettcher was therefore not of the opinion that the discrepancy between the ABO and DNA tests was as easily explained away as occurred at the original trial. He wrote three long reports that were tendered in evidence at the second appeal, as well as giving oral testimony to the effect that discrepancy between the two meant that DNA testing should be regarded as unreliable.

For Boettcher it simply comes down to this – the ABO testing on the semen stains taken from the red beach towel used to cover Celia's body in 1983 decisively excluded Butler as the donor of the sperm, and that the sperm came from a man with blood group O, whilst Wayne is blood group B.

He went further, criticising the testing procedures at the JTC, including the work by Freney. Boettcher claimed that the testing undertaken in 1997 actually mixed up the DNA taken from Wayne's blood with DNA extracted from the red towel.

The DNA extracted from the beach towel matched Butler's DNA. Boettcher claims that, according to his analysis of the records, DNA extracted from Wayne's blood stain was erroneously split into two, due to mislabelling of the test tubes, leading to the incorrect match as it would lead to the two samples having identical profiles as they both came from Butler.

I needed to clarify exactly what was going on with these samples, as the whole case rests on whether they were accurately, and reliably, analysed. I arranged to meet Professor Boettcher at his home in Newcastle, where his wife Moira provided a lovely lunch before we got down to the business of figuring out what was going on.

Barry had spent a considerable amount of time going through all the records. He showed me sample logs and the relevant DNA extractions sheets. The crux of the issue came down to when the sample semen stain was divided; either before testing or after. But from the records and other information, it's not possible to tell for sure.

Both cannot be true. And it makes a huge difference to how the evidence is evaluated.

Adding to the confusion is the fact that, if the sample of beach towel was split into two, it defied logic that one half came back providing strong results that match Butler's DNA, but the other half has consistently failed to return any result at all.

Cutting through the confusion, what this could mean is that, due to a laboratory error, samples that showed a match between Butler and the POI were both derived from DNA extracted from Butler's DNA sample – which is why they always return identical results – and the tests were never comparing the unknown contributor from the towel to Wayne.

Whatever the solution to this problem, the DNA evidence is inherently unreliable, and surely the conviction must be considered unsound because this is the only physical evidence against Butler. Everything else was circumstantial.

Mr R D Cavanagh, acting for Butler, suggested that Boettcher's expert reports given in evidence at the appeal meant that the 'evidence given by Freney at trial was potentially misleading and the conclusions scientifically flawed'.

Mrs Anjali Henders, another DNA expert from the John Tonge Centre involved in the DNA testing in early 1997, also gave evidence at the appeal. Although not called as a witness at trial in 2001, Henders now provided the court with details of the extraction process, which clarified the likelihood of contamination having occurred as Professor Boettcher suggested. In her evidence, Henders stated that although the test tubes are numbered sequentially, they were not processed in that order, as blood samples and semen samples are held in two separate racks. The blood sample was placed in a water bath as part of the DNA extraction technique before the beach towel was removed from the container before being divided between the two test tubes.

However, how reliable this testimony was is questionable, given Boettcher's claims that there were procedural errors with labelling at the JTC, which was substantiated during Butler's trial when staff from the Centre admitted making labelling errors during the DNA testing process, but maintained that the results were accurate.

Either way, any procedural error of this type can be grounds for an appeal, particularly when it calls into question the only physical evidence linking an accused to a crime.

But those weren't the only forensic tests undertaken on the beach towel.

In 2006 additional analyses were run. Again, DNA experts from the Division of Analytical Laboratories tested one of the two towel samples they were sent. Ms Samantha Cave, a forensic scientist at the John Tonge Centre, compared the resultant DNA profile obtained from the sample with that obtained from Butler's blood stain. Ms Cave said that 'the probability of this DNA profile occurring if the DNA present on the piece of red towel had come from someone other than Wayne Butler is approximately one in 200 thousand million (based on Queensland data)'.

Other very experienced experts were called to give evidence at the 2009 appeal, not least amongst them Mr Robert Goetz, the officer in charge of the Forensic Biology/DNA Laboratory in New South Wales for 20 years. Mr Goetz was recognised by the court as highly experienced. He examined the case notes produced by the analysts at the JTC, and concluded that Boettcher was incorrect in his contention that the 1983 ABO tests proved the donor of the sperm on the red beach towel was blood group O. Further, he said that had the analysis been undertaken by his laboratory, they would have reported the results as 'inconclusive'.

The judges concluded that the ABO grouping result obtained in 1983 cast doubt over the reliability of the DNA profiling analysis in 1997, because Professor Boettcher's opinion was at odds with the other DNA experts, but that the DNA testing performed in 1997 was not flawed even though it did not correspond with the earlier ABO test.

The appeal was eventually heard at the Court of Appeal in 2009. Justice Patrick Keane summed up the decision by the court by saying that it was not possible that the samples of red beach towel tested for DNA had been contaminated, dismissing Professor Boettcher's evidence, and that 'there has never been any suggestion that the semen found on the red towel might reasonably be thought not to be that of the killer of the deceased. I am satisfied that there is no reasonable doubt that Mr Butler's DNA was on the red towel found covering the body of the deceased when it was found on 2 September 1983. I therefore conclude, on the whole of the evidence, that Mr Butler was rightly convicted of having murdered the deceased'.

With that, Wayne's appeal was unanimously dismissed.

PROBLEMS IN QUEENSLAND

To decide how much weight should be attributed to Professor Boettcher's claims that mislabelling led to the allegedly erroneous DNA results, we need to look more closely at what was going on at the John Tonge Centre in Queensland, where the tests were carried out in 1997 and 2001.

In 2005, things were not going well for staff at the JTC, when an internal report by biologist Deanna Belzer was leaked to the *Courier Mail* newspaper. In the report, Belzer noted serious quality assurance concerns, inconsistent evidence results and huge backlogs.

The problems at the centre were well known, in terms of the logjam that had been created by the thousands of samples waiting to be tested, which was causing knock-on problems for the police and courts as they waited for evidence to be processed. As a result, arbitrary decisions were being made as to which samples to test first, in order to ensure 'major crimes' were prioritised. This also meant that large numbers of samples were never tested.

You can imagine the pressure staff were under to increase through flow to try to make a dent in the backlog, especially after a $5 million cash injection saw no improvements; in fact, in 2004 it was revealed that the 11,000 untested samples had grown to almost 14,000. Clearly, these problems had been developing for a while.

This was a major concern for the public, who rely on forensic laboratories to provide dependable and accurate results. Public expectations of high standards and timely turnarounds were falling well short.

As a result, an independent expert from New Zealand's Environmental Science and Research facility was brought in to review the quality and management of the work being undertaken at the centre. This review was meant to 'clear the air', and restore public confidence.

And this was desperately needed as, damningly, Belzer's leaked report also stated that she feared she and other staff were breaking the law by claiming DNA evidence produced by the centre was accurate when it may not have been.

Had this impacted the results of the tests undertaken in Celia Douty's murder? It is impossible to say. However, as Professor Boettcher is one of the country's leading DNA experts, and he has reviewed the processes undertaken at the time, a serious question has been raised over the validity of the evidence.

DNA EVIDENCE CAN ALSO EXONERATE THE WRONGLY CONVICTED

For those interested in miscarriages of justice, it seems like every day another person in the US is being exonerated on the basis of new DNA evidence proving they were not responsible for the crime for which they have been convicted.

The Innocence Project in the United States provides some pretty sobering statistics. Its website (www.innocenceproject.org) states that 367 people have been exonerated at the time of writing, 20 of whom were on death row. For various reasons, 41 of these people pleaded guilty to crimes they did not commit. The process of exoneration is slow – exonerees spend an average of 14 years in prison before their conviction is overturned, and those 367 people in total have spent 5097.5 years in prison for crimes for which they were innocent.

We have not seen as many cases in Australia, but clearly we are not immune to miscarriages of justice occurring.

A now infamous wrongful conviction is that of Frank Button, who was convicted of raping a 13-year-old girl in Queensland in 1999, and was sentenced to serve six years in prison. Initially the young victim said she did not know who had raped her but gave a description. She later changed her statement, naming Button as her attacker. DNA evidence was not included in the case against Button, as sperm collected as part of the forensic examination of Celia's remains failed to provide conclusive DNA results as to the donor.

Bedding from the crime scene was also sent to the lab, but these were not tested because of the victim's identification of Button, as well as expert evidence given by a DNA scientist who stated at trial that 'no conclusive results could be gleaned from vaginal swab DNA testing'.

Button then lodged an appeal, based on the absence of scientific evidence against him. Although there was no statutory right for a defendant to be able to insist on DNA analysis being undertaken in an attempt to demonstrate innocence at the post-conviction stage, Button's defence team were insistent – they understood the power of DNA evidence in this context to exonerate.

At this stage, the bedding was tested and a semen stain discovered – the resultant DNA profile did not match Button. The vaginal swabs from the rape kit were then retested, and a male DNA profile obtained. This didn't match Button either, but did match the DNA recovered from the bedsheets.

When the DNA profile was run against the convicted offender DNA database, it matched a man already serving time for rape, who matched the victim's original description and who was living in the community at the time of the offence.

Frank Button was subsequently released in 2001, but not before he had spent 10 months in prison where he had been physically and sexually assaulted. The Queensland Court of Criminal Appeal labelled this 'a black day in the history of criminal justice administration in Australia'.

This was the first case in which DNA analysis was used to free a wrongfully convicted person in Australia.

Worryingly, the initial DNA work undertaken to obtain a DNA profile from the vaginal swab was done at the JTC – the same lab that analysed the DNA exhibits in Butler's case in 1997.

Judge Williams, as part of Button's 2001 appeal, was scathing in the judgment summary:

What is disturbing is that the investigating authorities had also taken possession of bedding from the bed on which the offence occurred, and delivered those exhibits to the John Tonge Centre. No testing of that bedding was carried out prior to trial. The explanation given was that it would not be of material assistance in identifying the appellant as the perpetrator of the crime.

That is true in a sense, but of course DNA testing has a two-fold purpose: that of identifying the perpetrator of a crime, and secondly, that of excluding a possible offender as being the perpetrator of the crime.

When evidence focuses solely on guilt testing, to the exclusion of innocence testing, miscarriages of justice occur.

In this instance, a man spent 10 months in prison for no reason at all, except someone arbitrarily decided that evidence should not be tested.

And it came back to the backlog at the JTC. The Director of Public Prosecutions, in her submissions to the appeal court, noted the fact that the centre was under-resourced, and court processes had been held up because testing had not been completed. There were also more questions about the quality of the work being carried out, as the expert who had stated at trial that vaginal swabs could not yield viable DNA profiles was also based at the JTC. Clearly, this assertion was later proven to be untrue.

The ripples of the problems in Queensland continued to spread. At least one man was wrongfully convicted because of work not done or inconclusive tests, of that we can be sure.

But how many more miscarriages of justice can also be linked to this dark time in forensic science provision?

THE LEGAL FIGHT TO FREE WAYNE BUTLER

Many people believe that when there is a DNA 'match' it's a slam dunk. No so.

DNA evidence can be unreliable for a number of reasons. Firstly, evidence can be inadvertently contaminated; i.e. the introduction of something into a sample that was not originally there. This can occur at the scene, during collection, at the lab during testing, and whilst in storage. Many people can contaminate the evidence – victims, witnesses, suspects, emergency responders, crime scene investigators and lab technicians.

Contamination is a major source of concern for forensic

scientists, as one hint that evidence may be unreliable and the case can fall apart.

Secondly, DNA evidence in the form of blood or other body fluid can be introduced to a scene intentionally, i.e. evidence can be planted (we'll see this in the case of Scott Austic in chapter six).

Thirdly, as we have seen in Butler's case, DNA evidence can also be interpreted in different ways. Even when evidence is as readily accepted as DNA, as we have seen, problems can arise. And I am always concerned with a conviction where only one type of evidence is used to convict someone, especially when the stakes are so high, as in murder and sexual assault cases.

There has to be corroboration. That could take the form of additional forensic or circumstantial evidence, or eyewitness testimony. But something.

The University of New South Wales Council for Civil Liberties summed the problem up nicely in a briefing paper entitled *DNA Evidence, Wrongful Conviction and Wrongful Acquittals*, stating, 'As DNA evidence cannot prove all the elements of an offence, it cannot therefore prove of itself that someone is guilty beyond reasonable doubt.'

The fight goes on.

In November 2016, Butler applied to the Governor of Queensland, Paul de Jersey, for a pardon, as he had always maintained his innocence. A detailed application comprising some 80 pages across two volumes, and largely based on Boettcher's findings in regards to inconsistencies with the DNA evidence against Wayne, was passed to Attorney General Yvette D'Ath. Again, Butler was unsuccessful. The response from the Governor's Official Secretary in October 2017 simply advised that '. . . I am directed to inform you that there is no justification for the exercise of any powers conferred on His Excellency by the Constitution of Queensland 2001 in this case'.

No information was provided regarding the grounds for this decision.

In April 2017, Boettcher wrote to Mr Ian Stewart, Commissioner of Police, Queensland, making claims of perjury against staff at the John Tonge Centre, namely Freney and Henders, based on the evidence they gave at Butler's original murder trial and appeal, which he says is in direct conflict with the lab notes of the samples that were tested. This was a serious accusation, but one Boettcher was willing to make given that he believes Butler would not have been convicted without their version of events – i.e. that the towel was split *before* the two halves were extracted separately for DNA. Boettcher is of the opinion that both Freney and Henders knew that they were lying, but were doing so to cover an error.

On 1 June the matter was passed to Detective Sergeant Kite, of the Homicide Investigation Unit of the Queensland Police Service. On 12 January and again on 25 April 2018, Boettcher followed up with Kite, as it had been over 12 months since he had submitted his complaint of perjury to Mr Stewart.

In July 2018 Kite sent Professor Boettcher an email advising that no action would be taken in regard to the complaint of perjury. Further, he had found that '. . . there is no evidence to suggest either person committed perjury'.

Boettcher responded by email, stating that Kite's conclusion was not supported by the information and documentation provided. He asked for a response from Kite in order to appreciate how Kite had reached his conclusion. No further communication has been received.

THE OUTCOME

Wayne Butler has been released on parole, which he will remain on indefinitely. Even so, his supporters have not given up the fight against his conviction.

Professor Barry Boettcher is concise in his summing up of the situation: 'I can't say if Wayne Butler murdered Celia Douty; all I can say is that the laboratory results are wrong. This is a case of wrongful conviction – it was not Butler's semen on the towel.'

If this is true, there are serious ramifications.

Firstly, this means a man languished in prison for a murder he did not commit, and lost 18 years of his life. Worse, he will remain formally guilty of murder until the error is rectified.

Secondly, Celia's murderer remains at large, and given the violence and random nature of the crime, would have still been a danger to the community and may have gone on to commit more crimes.

Thirdly, this case is heralded as a landmark in the use of DNA to catch an offender. The advent of DNA profiling in 1997 revolutionised the science of human identification, and the concern is that if the DNA analysis in this case is unreliable, that will call into question a very significant number of other prosecutions based on the same technology; especially those that were prosecuted contemporaneously with Butler and using DNA samples analysed at the JTC.

IN THE END . . .

This case is still making news, with one 2019 *Herald Sun* headline reading 'How a semen stain "solved" the Brampton Island murder but "left a killer at large"'.

I don't know whether Wayne Butler is innocent or not; only Butler and the actual offender (if not Butler) know that. But as a forensic scientist, what concerns me about this case, even if we accept the DNA evidence as reliable, is that a man was found guilty of murder based on one type of evidence alone; as apart from Butler having opportunity, the only evidence against him was the DNA evidence on the beach towel.

Clearly Professor Boettcher wants the evidence provided by Freney and Henders to be compared with the records in the case files, and for this to be undertaken in a court of law, as he concludes that Butler has been convicted on unreliable evidence.

Butler is lucky to have someone as knowledgeable as Barry on his side, as it can be very difficult for people – especially those in prison – to know what processes to follow to seek redress if they are claiming to be wrongly accused. In this case, for example, many of the copies of laboratory records that are relevant were obtained only after the 2009 Appeal by an application made under Right To Information legislation, which Butler applied for himself before he sent the files to Boettcher in 2012.

One person that would disagree that this case requires further examination is former Mackay detective, Andre Wijtenburg, the man responsible for re-opening the case against Butler in 1996 when he learnt that advances in DNA technology could solve Celia's murder.

Wijtenburg is unswerving in his belief that Butler is guilty, telling a newspaper in 2017 that 'I am 100 per cent confident we have got the right guy'.

He also stated that the DNA evidence had been challenged a number of times, and had stood up. He was sure, if challenged again, the result would be the same.

Whichever side of the fence you are on, whether you think Wayne Butler is innocent or guilty, there is only one way to answer the question once and for all.

As a result, I would like to see the DNA from the red beach towel re-tested by an independent laboratory, and the results compared to a new sample taken from Butler. If it's a match, then the issues over testing at John Tonge Centre are no longer of relevance – to this case at least, the wider implications remain. If the results of the comparison between the beach towel and Butler do not match, then the DNA from the towel should be uploaded to the DNA database, to determine if a person known to the police was the originator of the semen, and therefore also the person who killed Celia. Of course, if that scenario were to ensue, Butler's conviction should then be quashed.

But I will not be holding my breath that this will happen, and it is not clear if any of the original beach towel with semen staining remains to be re-tested.

Also of serious concern were the procedural problems at the John Tonge Centre, and I do wonder how many other cases have been compromised as a result of inaccurate record-keeping or unreliable sample testing/comparison. Until the issue of the sample testing is resolved, Butler's conviction could be argued to be unsound.

This case also speaks to the bigger problem of backlogs in the testing of forensic samples, and the almost arbitrary selection of which exhibits take precedence.

And the problem remains. For example, there are literally thousands of rape kits waiting to be processed across all states and territories in Australia, which means victims are not being given justice after being sexually assaulted, and offenders are free to roam the streets, possibly attacking more people.

To give you an idea of scale, since 2012, according to information obtained from the New South Wales Police Force, 1053 kits have not been tested. This of a total of 5243, with 3627 having been tested; the remaining 563 were not accounted for in either group. This is not what the public expects from our criminal justice system.

We know that when kits are tested, results are achieved. In 2019, a news report stated that grants made available for clearing backlogs in rape kit testing across 20 US states allowed 55,000 tests to be undertaken. Some of the kits had been sitting unanalysed for years.

As a result of that injection of funds, 165 prosecutions have taken place and 64 convictions have been achieved.

Clearing the DNA backlogs for serious cases in Australia, and increasing the ability to process more samples more quickly to avoid the lottery of decision-making that currently takes place must surely be priorities for the federal government. Otherwise, what justice is there for victims of serious crimes, or the wrongly accused?

TWO

KELVIN CONDREN:
THE COERCED CONFESSION
(1983)

'The most significant contributing factor bringing
Aboriginal people into conflict with the criminal justice
system was their disadvantaged and unequal position in
the wider society.'
The Royal Commission into Aboriginal Deaths in Custody 1991

Mount Isa is a hot, dry place. An isolated mining city, located
around 1800 kilometres north-west of Brisbane and 1200 kilometres south-west of Cairns, it has a population of around 21,000
people and a lot of social problems, including crime rates running
at four times the state average, a phenomenon that can be partially
explained by the high unemployment and relatively low social-
economic status of the area in general, as well as a large itinerant
population. To give context, in 2012 there were two murders and
more than 600 assaults, making Mount Isa the most violent city in
Queensland on a per capita basis.

On a trip to Brisbane in 2019, I took a detour to Mount Isa,
as I was preparing my notes on this chapter and wanted to see for

myself where the crime happened and to get a sense of the culture and people who live in this tough, remote place. Looking out over the town, you feel the sense of isolation. Grey chimney stacks stand clear above the township, silhouetted against a deep blue sky, surrounded by dry grassland and red dirt.

Mount Isa and the surrounding lands are home to the Kalkadoon people, and there is a large Aboriginal population in the area. Against this backdrop of social deprivation and hardship, in the 1980s there was a pattern of endemic police racism. So when young Aboriginal woman Patricia Carlton was violently murdered, the police soon zoned in on an easy target – Indigenous man Kelvin Condren. There was no forensic or eyewitness evidence linking Kelvin to the attack, nor any motive.

The police had one thing – Kelvin's confession.

I simply cannot understand how a confession alone – especially a retracted confession – could lead to a man being found guilty of murder. If Condren had murdered Patricia, especially in a such a brutal way, why, when he was arrested later, was he not covered in blood? Yet the police did not collect or produce at trial a single scrap of physical or forensic evidence linking him to Patricia's murder.

The jury, however, was convinced by the prosecution's case, and Condren was found guilty of murder and jailed for life. There are two problems with this: 1) Condren had an alibi, and 2) someone else – a violent predator – confessed to the murder one month after Condren's arrest and before he was taken to trial.

Later, because of the determination of a journalist to find the truth and draw public attention to Condren's plight, it became apparent that Condren had a water-tight alibi and his conviction was quashed in 1991. In 1995 he was offered $400,000 as compensation for his wrongful conviction.

This case not only saw an innocent man go to prison for six

years, but the victim's murder remains formally 'unsolved', so her family has never been given the closure it deserves and there has never been any justice for Patricia.

The murder of an Aboriginal woman by an Aboriginal man in the mid-1980s in outback Queensland made few headlines. As a result, this case not only reflects injustice for those immediately involved, but raises issues of prejudice that are still reflected in today's criminal justice system – another core theme of miscarriages of justice that we will, sadly, see again and again.

THE CASE

Kelvin Condren was a 22-year-old unemployed Aboriginal man who moved to Mount Isa in late August or early September 1983. He soon began a relationship with 24-year-old Patricia Carlton. They had only been seeing each other for about three weeks when Patricia was killed.

On the afternoon of Friday 30 September 1983, Kelvin and Patricia had been drinking with friends at the Mount Isa Hotel. When Kelvin left the hotel around 5:45pm, he was arrested for drunkenness and held in the cells overnight.

Patricia was found at 5:40am on Saturday morning by a routine police patrol, in the car park behind the Mount Isa Hotel. She was alive, but very badly injured. According to the police, Patricia had been attacked on the Friday around 4:15pm, and had lain unconscious in the car park until the early hours of the next day. It did not appear that she had been assaulted and then moved. She had been brutally beaten around the head with a metal pipe, and a large stone had been inserted into her vagina.

Patricia was taken to Mount Isa Hospital, but she later succumbed to her injuries. She had never regained consciousness, so there was no opportunity for her to tell anyone who had attacked her.

Meanwhile, Kelvin had been sobering up in the cells. After he was released from the Mount Isa watchhouse on Saturday 1 October, he resumed drinking with his friends at a dry creek bed.

By this stage the police had begun to investigate the attack on Patricia, and had been told that Kelvin had been with her for a short period before the assault. The police began to check the regular drinking spots around Mount Isa, and at around 12:30pm they found Condren on the dry creek bed with about 12 other people. Kelvin was taken back to the police station, as he was already suspected in the attack on Patricia.

At this point, Condren didn't know Patricia had been assaulted, but once questioning began, the truth soon dawned on him. Allegedly, before he was even formally interviewed, Kelvin confessed to the attack.

Whilst the police were questioning Kelvin, they were also interviewing the people he and Patricia had been drinking with on that Friday afternoon.

Once the news of Patricia's death was received at the police station, Condren's original charge of attempted murder was upgraded to murder.

Kelvin took part in a formal police interview, in the presence of a Justice of the Peace (JP). According to police, Condren again confessed to Patricia's murder during this interview.

The police interviewed a number of Kelvin and Patricia's friends, including Louise Brown and Stephen McNamee (de facto husband and wife), who both gave statements. McNamee stated that he had witnessed Condren assaulting Patricia, and Brown that Kelvin had admitted to them that he had 'damaged' Patricia. Another witness, Fabian Butcher, a relative of Patricia's, gave a statement to say that on the morning after the attack on Patricia, Condren told him he had 'bashed up' a girl with a stick.

None of the witness statements taken by police were used in evidence against him because within days of the statements being taken, several witnesses had made allegations their police statements were false. By the time Condren's committal hearing began in December 1983, Brown and McNamee both refused to adopt their statements, claiming they were false and made under duress. Only one person, Fabian Butcher, was still available to give evidence against Condren at the committal hearing that matched his original statement, but he did not give evidence at the murder trial because he was found dead on 16 April, having committed suicide by hanging.

Kelvin's trial began on 6 August 1984. After just nine days of hearings, on 15 August he was convicted of murdering Patricia, on the basis of his signed 'confession' (whilst he continually maintained this was obtained under duress), and he was jailed for life.

I have to wonder, if Condren had been a white man with a steady job who had not been drinking heavily, would the jury have seen – and judged – him differently? Would they have expected some actual evidence or witnesses of actual physical harm, and a motive, linking him to Patricia's death before they would have been willing to find him guilty of murder beyond reasonable doubt?

Condren appealed his conviction through the Queensland Court of Criminal Appeal. The appeal ran from March to May 1987, with 'fresh' evidence being called; this comprised the Crown witnesses alleging that their evidence was obtained improperly under duress and apparent sightings of Patricia after the time of death given by police (around 4:15pm).

Two new witnesses, Wesley Kenny and Judy McConachie, gave evidence at the appeal. They had been drinking at Mount Isa Hotel on 30 September and said Patricia was there until at least 7:40pm – at least two and a half hours after Condren had been picked up for drunkenness and safely housed at the Mount Isa watch house.

Also tendered in evidence was linguistic expert Dr Diana Eades' analysis of the speech patterns in Condren's Record of Interview (which was meant to be a true written record of questions asked and answers given in response during a formal police interview word-for-word, and was the document used to convict him). Dr Eades analysed the grammatical structures and ways of communicating in the formal police interview as compared to other interviews that had been recorded of Condren in other legal contexts, based on an understanding of language patterns by Aboriginal people speaking English.

Dr Eades' evaluation supported the hypothesis that the answers given by Condren in his formal statement had not been typed verbatim as the police had claimed, as they did not match Kelvin's normal speech patterns, casting serious doubt on the authorship of the confession evidence and lending weight to the allegation that the confession was fabricated.

On 8 May the appeal court rejected the application, commenting that the eyewitness evidence was not 'new' as it was available and should have been heard at the original trial. As a result, the evidence of the two new eyewitnesses who claimed they saw Patricia in the bar at the hotel until at least 7:40pm was dismissed as lacking credibility, as it was inconsistent with evidence given by other witnesses.

The other main focus of the appeal had been the expert evidence given by Dr Eades, which tended to support Kelvin's claims that his confession was coerced. However, the appeal judges determined that Dr Eades' opinion 'usurped the role of the jury'. The judges also failed to recognise forensic linguistics as a specialised field of knowledge, a requirement for evidence to be declared admissible. As a result, Dr Eades' expert opinion was declared legally inadmissible.

EXPERT INSERT: FORENSIC LINGUISTICS

Forensic linguistics is different from many of the other forensic sciences because linguistics is a social science. Social scientists work on systematic development of logic and evidence to understand human behaviour in its social settings, including particular groups (e.g. social, cultural, community, professional) and institutions (e.g. law, education, health). The human behaviour that linguists study is communication, primarily through language, whether spoken, written, or signed.

Like other sciences, forensic linguists' work is empirical. We focus on what people say/write/sign in actual situations. Whilst there is some experimental linguistics, much linguistic work does not start with hypotheses, but with observations of language use, typically audio- or video-recorded. The close study and documentation of patterns of language enable linguists to confirm and disconfirm generalisations about these patterns, which leads to tentative hypotheses, tested with further language data. Theory is developed as a result of this inductive process. The ultimate aim of linguistic analysis, as with other social sciences, is not proof but understanding; about what is arguably the most complex data for any scientific analysis, namely patterned ways of acting within the complexity of human social behaviour.

In the mid-1980s, forensic linguistics was very new in Australia, although there had been an important use of it back in 1959. Rupert Stuart was an Arrernte man (a group of Aboriginal Australians that live at Mparntwe – Alice Springs – and surrounding areas of the Central region of the NT) in his 20s, convicted and sentenced to hang for the murder of nine-year-old Mary Hattan in December 1958. The evidence against Stuart comprised largely a signed confession, which he claimed was coerced as a result of police brutality. Stuart neither read nor wrote in English, and indeed his spoken English was also very poor, and therefore he could not have dictated the confession in the manner the police claimed at the original trial, which was written in clear and sophisticated English. Like the cases in this book, Stuart had a champion – Catholic priest Father Tom Dixon, who originally attended Adelaide prison to prepare Stuart for his execution. Dixon soon came to believe Stuart was not guilty, and took up the fight to save his life. As part of this battle, Dixon sought out anthropologist and linguist Ted Strehlow, who had been brought up in Arrernte society and had known Stuart for many years. Strehlow then undertook the first ever evaluation of Aboriginal English as compared to standard Australian English. His analysis demonstrated that Stuart could not have spoken the words as written in the alleged confession. The media then took up Stuart's cause, and petitions with thousands of signatures called for his sentence to be commuted. There were many appeals, and eventually his sentence was commuted to life imprisonment. He was eventually released on parole in 1973. One man's life ruined, as the result of a coerced confession, but the repercussions were much larger – Stuart's predicament was really the first to draw attention to the problems Aboriginal people face in court in Australia. In addition, this case had a significant part to play in the abolition of the death penalty in South Australia, as people realised the consequences for those wrongly accused or prosecuted on unreliable evidence.

Even though they occurred decades apart, a clear parallel can be drawn between Rupert and Kelvin's cases: a vulnerable, Indigenous suspect, and alleged police brutality to achieve a coerced confession.

In Condren's case, the linguistic evidence centred on dialectal differences between Queensland Aboriginal English and Australian English. Linguists in the 1960s had discovered that Aboriginal English is a dialect like Scottish English or African American English. However, in the mid-1980s when forensic linguistic evidence was given in Condren's case, there was still little understanding outside linguistics of Aboriginal English as a systematic dialect that is different from other dialects of English. And comments from the appeal judges in this case also revealed how widespread was the mistaken belief that only Aboriginal people with dark skin would speak a linguistically recognised distinct dialect of English.

The linguistic evidence in Condren's case centred on his answers in the typed police record of interview, allegedly taken down 'word-for-word'. My analysis revealed a striking difference between the answers attributed to Condren to the 155 questions in this police interview on the one hand, with his answers to questions in both his Supreme Court trial, and in an interview I conducted with him in prison, on the other hand. For example, interviews in the legal process organise the telling of events chronologically, and clock time plays an important role. In contrast, in the 1980s it was much more common for Aboriginal people to structure the telling of events in terms of people and place, and for many, clock time was irrelevant. (This is still true for many Aboriginal people.) But the answer attributed to Condren to the question 'When did you do this?' was 'Quarter past four.' My expert opinion provided overwhelming evidence that this, and several other linguistic patterns in answers attributed to Condren, were inconsistent with his other analysed interviews and what was known to characterise Aboriginal English.

In the decades since Condren's case, the field of forensic linguistics has grown considerably and a range of linguistic methods is employed in answering diverse questions in expert opinions for courts. The issue of fabricated confessions is no longer relevant because of the mandatory recording of police interviews with suspects, beginning in the early 1990s. But an important question can arise about a suspect's comprehension of the right to remain silent, including the consequences of waiving that right. Detailed linguistic analysis of the police questions and suspect answers often sheds a light on features of talk that may have not been noticed by non-linguistically trained people. Linguistic analysis cannot prove comprehension or non-comprehension. But research discoveries about what makes legal language hard to understand, and about the complexities of learning and using a second language, can be essential bases to the forensic linguist's analysis of a police interview that leads to an opinion provided to assist the judge or jury in making a decision.

Dr Diana Eades, Adjunct Professor in the Department of Linguistics at the University of New England

In short, this meant that the Court of Criminal Appeal was totally rejecting evidence that should, at the very least, have raised serious concerns about Condren's guilt.

As a result, for a while, it appeared as if that would be the end of the story, and Condren would remain in prison for a crime he did not commit.

However, the media proved itself Kelvin's friend, largely through the efforts of investigative journalist Chris Masters, who in March 1988 ran a penetrating piece on the case for Channel Ten's news and current affairs program, *Page One*. Two people who the producers had located were Mr Price, a pharmacist at Menzies Pharmacy in Mount Isa, and his employee Ms Millican. They stated in the documentary that the murder could not have been committed at 4:15pm on the Friday evening as the police believed – they were sure, as their pharmacy was next to the car park where Patricia was found and both had walked separately across the car park; Millican at 5:15pm and Price at 5:45pm, both in broad daylight. They were categorical that Patricia was not lying in the car park when they passed through.

This was crucial evidence, as, if we accept it as accurate (and we have no reason not to), it means that 1) the police had the time of the attack wrong; Patricia could not have been assaulted before 5:45pm, and 2) by extension, Kelvin had an incontrovertible alibi – he was being held in a police cell overnight, having been arrested by the police for being drunken and disorderly at 5:47pm, about 200 metres away from the crime scene.

At the time of his arrest, Condren had been so drunk he had needed assistance getting into the police van, so there is no way he could have violently attacked Patricia immediately after Price passed through the car park at 5:45pm, and got 200 metres up the road to be picked up by police barely able to stand unassisted at 5:47pm. This would have given Kelvin two minutes to perform a violent and sustained assault and then run 200 metres up the road to where the police found him, somehow without any blood on him. It was simply impossible.

You might be wondering why Price and Millican did not come forward before, as clearly their evidence could have saved an innocent man spending over six years in prison. Well, firstly the case was not big news in Mount Isa – on Monday 3 October, *The North West Star*, the local newspaper, simply noted that a man had appeared in the Magistrate's Court charged with murder. Unless they were following the case closely, which Price and Millican weren't (Price had gone on an overseas holiday the morning after the attack), they would have had no reason to know their information regarding the time they crossed the car park would be key to providing Kelvin with a watertight alibi.

Neither had been interviewed by the police during the original investigation into Patricia's death, nor were they called as witnesses at Kelvin's trial, which means the police did not do a thorough canvass of the area looking for witnesses to the crime, or other contributions that could have helped clarify what had happened.

But Kelvin's legal team was unsure what could be done, because although Condren clearly had a case, as this was new evidence, Queensland law only allows for one appeal, and that avenue had already been tried and the appeal rejected.

Kelvin's legal team presented this new evidence to the Queensland Governor at the time, Sir Walter Campbell, petitioning him to pardon Condren on the basis of further fresh evidence (i.e. the witnesses from the pharmacy), but he declined to act.

Following Campbell's refusal to pardon Condren, in November 1989, Condren's defence team made an application to lodge an Appeal to the High Court, but the High Court determined that it could not hear new evidence on appeal. However, the justices did comment that they found the new witness evidence 'Relevant, cogent and plausible', whilst also suggesting that the Queensland Crown reconsider its position.

In the meantime, the Attorney General for the Northern Territory wrote to the Queensland Attorney General, Paul Clauson, describing further confessions by another man to two psychiatrists (we'll refer to this man as Mr A for now, as this is what the Criminal Justice Commission called him, however we will introduce him properly shortly, as his identity is now known).

Then the wait resumed as the matter was adjourned, whilst Paul Clauson decided what, if anything, should be done. Another let down; Clauson determined that he would not refer the case to the Court of Criminal Appeal.

The Queensland legal authorities appeared determined to ignore the problems with the case, and in the face of mounting evidence that Kelvin could not have murdered Patricia, maintained their intransigent attitude.

Still, Condren and his legal team didn't give up, and immediately lodged an Application to Appeal to the High Court against the decision, as enough people were now fighting to ensure that the Queensland Crown would not be allowed to simply ignore the obvious injustice.

In November 1989 the Director of Public Prosecutions, Des Sturgess QC, stated that he would speak to the Attorney General about the new evidence.

At last, the legal system did not let Kelvin down. On 6 December 1989, five and a half years after Kelvin was sent to prison for murder, the new Attorney General of Queensland, Dean Wells, announced that Kelvin's Petition for Pardon would be referred to the Court of Criminal Appeal as a result of the fresh evidence. Important to note is that this happened just after a state election, and the Labor Party had promised to reopen Condren's case, if elected.

It took another six months, but on 26 June 1990, the Court of Criminal Appeal set aside Kelvin's murder conviction on the grounds that it was unsafe, and ordered a retrial, commenting that a miscarriage of justice had occurred and this would remain the status quo unless the evidence of three new witnesses not heard during the original trial was presented in front of a jury. The retrial never happened. Instead, the new Director of Public Prosecutions, Royce Miller QC, prepared a report for the Attorney General stating that a *nolle prosequi* (a Latin phrase, and when applied in a legal setting, amounts to 'do not prosecute') should be entered on the charge against Condren – in essence meaning all charges should be dropped.

As a result, the charge of murder against Condren was withdrawn in the Supreme Court on 27 July 1990. After over six years in prison, Kelvin was free, and no longer wrongly labelled a murderer. But he was not going to let the injustice be forgotten.

POST-CONVICTION COMPLAINTS

Following his release, Kelvin and three of the witnesses who gave prosecution evidence at his trial – Louise Brown, Stephen McNamee, and Noreen Jumbo – made complaints against the Queensland Police Service (QPS) to the Criminal Justice Commission (CJC), established in 1989 and now the Crime and Corruption Commission, brought into effect with the *Criminal Justice Act* of 1989 and the remit of which is to monitor, review, co-ordinate and initiate reform of the administration of criminal justice in Queensland. One of the CJC's core functions is to investigate allegations of misconduct against QPS, which is what the scope of this inquiry was limited to; the purpose was never to determine who killed Patricia.

The CJC had the power to conduct investigative hearings, and whilst much of the information that would be heard had been picked over in various courts over the preceding years, the Commission could also hear evidence that would have been inadmissible in a criminal court.

Kelvin and McNamee's complaints were perhaps the most serious due to the allegations of physical assault by police, but all spoke of police corruption. This fitted exactly within the newly established Commission's responsibilities, as three of its aims and objectives were:

- 'exposing corruption and official misconduct through hearings and reports to Parliament;
- providing evidence which leads to the prosecution of persons engaged in corruption or official misconduct, either before the courts, the Misconduct Tribunals or by disciplinary proceedings;
- reducing the incidence of misconduct, official misconduct and corruption in the police service and other units of public administration'.

Kelvin claimed, in a 25-page document, that the police investigating him for Patricia's murder created a false document in which a confession was attributed to him, namely the Record of Interview, that was later used against him in court. His complaint was founded on two key points. Firstly, the fact that the police allegedly subjected him to intimidation and assaulted before taking part in the formal interview in order to obtain the alleged confession, as well as his signature on the now disputed document, which was largely created by Queensland Police. Condren's second point was that the manner in which the police investigated Patricia's murder was prejudicial, inadequate, and inefficient.

In relation to the violence Kelvin said he was subjected to, he claimed to have been struck in the face with a telephone book. He did not complain about the injuries he alleged were the result of police brutality before he made his formal statement. This is hardly surprising, and does not indicate Kelvin was now lying – could we really expect Condren to make a complaint to a person working for the same organisation that assaulted him? This would potentially only have made things worse, and so Kelvin kept quiet.

But he also didn't complain to either his first solicitor, or the barrister who represented him at his committal hearing. Again, I don't find this suspicious – instead, I can quite easily understand how a man who has been set-up by the police for a murder he did not commit would be sceptical of any person involved with the criminal justice system, even those apparently there to help him.

But his claims, when taken into consideration alongside the witness statements of coercion, were taken seriously by the Commission. However, the Commission also had to consider that there was a Justice of the Peace present when Kelvin gave his Record of Interview, which should (in theory) have offered Condren protection.

Originally, and in a number of interviews, the JP denied Kelvin was prompted during questioning. However, the Justice of the Peace later agreed in evidence to the CJC that the police did 'prompt' answers from Kelvin, but that when Kelvin did answer questions, the answers were recorded accurately. The JP went on to say there were no occasions where Condren did not answer at all and a response was then fabricated by QPS, or that any answers given by Kelvin were then manipulated in the record to reflect the opposite of what Kelvin had actually said.

But, if we consider the fact that Condren was claiming the police were violent and coercive prior to the interview being formally recorded, we would expect his answers to conform to the police's desired outcomes. In essence we're left with two alternatives, either Kelvin was coached, and he gave the answers the police wanted under duress and fear of further violence, or his actual words were misrepresented.

The CJC agreed that the clear 'prompting' was troubling, as any omission of prompting or clarifying questions in a formal Record of Interview is intolerable in a criminal investigation – the stakes could not be higher for the accused, as it is this document upon which prosecution cases can be based, as in Kelvin's situation. So any evidence of police coercion could signify that a miscarriage of justice occurred.

The Commission was not willing to go that far in Kelvin's case, however. Taking into consideration the fact the JP changed his version of events a number of times, as well as the inconsistencies (however easily explained) in Condren's statements, the CJC stated that the evidence available did not support a decision to report the matter for consideration of either criminal or disciplinary charges against the officers involved. Condren's complaint of police coercion was therefore rejected.

But what about the second point, that the investigation was not fair, and was both inadequate and inefficient? One of the key issues here was that one month after Kelvin's arrest and *before* Kelvin's committal hearing, another man, Mr A, confessed to murdering an Aboriginal woman in late September 1983 in Mount Isa, whilst passing through on a bus trip, in similar circumstances to those in which Patricia was killed. This person was already in prison in the Northern Territory for another murder.

And Mr A's confession did demonstrate knowledge about the attack; he described how he had hit the Indigenous woman with a piece of pipe, and how he had inserted a rock into her vagina. He told the police that he spent around 30 minutes assaulting the victim (who we know must have been Patricia, as no other attacks of this nature and ferocity were reported in Mount Isa in September 1983), before he got on a Greyhound bus leaving for Katherine, which left at around 7:30pm (although it could have been later, as his movements were never fully investigated or confirmed).

This fits with the evidence of a Ms Little, manager of Menzies Pharmacy, who left work later than her two colleagues, Mr Price and Ms Millican. She walked across the car park where Patricia was attacked around 7:40pm–7:45pm that Friday evening. She said that, as she walked to her car, she heard moaning or gurgling, but dismissed it as coming from a drunk person. But, importantly, she also noted a bar lying on the ground near her car, which would correspond with Mr A's account.

This was a random assault, but from what Mr A said, this was clearly a crime that fitted the circumstances of Patricia's murder.

Mr A was in prison in Darwin when he made this confession, and in January 1984 a senior police officer involved in Patricia's murder investigation travelled to the NT to interview him, but at this point Mr A refused to cooperate.

The CJC did agree that the unnecessary delay between the confession and the officer travelling to the NT and attempting to interview Mr A was unhelpful. However, there was not enough evidence to show that the officer intentionally delayed in arranging the interview, and the CJC felt the delay in travel was caused by the logistical requirement of the travel being formally approved.

Mr A was called as a witness at Kelvin's trial, but refused to repeat his confession of murdering a woman in Mount Isa. He did admit to being in the town at the time of the attack on Patricia, and to drinking at the hotel there on 30 September 1983. He also told the court that he had punched an Aboriginal woman a number of times that night, and had left her where the assault had taken place. However, there appears to be general consensus that Mr A was heavily sedated the day he gave evidence at Condren's trial, and he was therefore unlikely to be a compelling witness to the jury as he was far from coherent. This may have affected how the jury felt about the reliability of his evidence in general, and diminished in their minds the potential weight of his earlier confession.

After his appearance at Condren's original trial, Mr A had made an additional, out-of-court statement confirming he was responsible for Patricia's death. Kelvin's defence argued that if the jury had heard of A's second confession there would have been a significant possibility of an acquittal.

I remain sceptical about the final point, as A had made such a disjointed impression on the jury, that the backwards and forwards between confessing and retracting made him inherently unreliable.

The Northern Territory Police and the Crown law officers were keen to assist with Condren's trial, and provided information quickly to their colleagues in Queensland, as well as expediting Mr A's murder trial so that he could be called as a Crown witness in Condren's case. But the detectives from QPS were not as speedy in their gathering of the information, and three months after Mr A's confession they had not collected information on his offences, which would have facilitated a comparison of the modus operandi between Patricia and Mr A's victim's murders.

Condren's counsel raised further complaints focused on the police's failure to interview other witnesses who may have supported Kelvin's version of events, and specifically if Patricia had been seen in the bar after Kelvin's arrest for drunkenness. These included bar staff and other customers at the hotel.

Another problem was that both Stephen McNamee and Louise Brown claimed that the statements taken by Queensland Police investigating the attack on Patricia were also coerced.

On 24 September 1990, Brown complained to the CJC that on 1 October 1983, when she was questioned, the police insisted that she make a statement saying she had witnessed Condren attacking Patricia with a steel bar behind the Mount Isa Hotel. Brown claimed that she was not present, and had not witnessed any assault, but had been coerced into signing the statement anyway.

Louise said that, aside from the personal information, the witness statement was entirely fabricated. This was not the first time Brown had stated that her statement was fictitious. On 3 October 1983, she had complained to the Aboriginal Legal Service (or ALS, now the Aboriginal & Torres Strait Islander Legal Service [Qld] Ltd) that her statement was false, but her de facto husband, McNamee, indicated that Brown did this because of fear of 'pay-back' by Patricia's family because Brown was (according to Condren's 'confession') one of a group of witnesses to the attack, but did not intervene or report it to the police.

Due to inconsistencies in the evidence about why Brown made the complaint to the ALS in 1983, the CJC could not use that to support the conclusion that Brown's police statement had been fabricated.

Stephen McNamee made a statement to the CJC that the police forced him to make false statements implicating Condren in Patricia's assault, through violence and threats. The police obviously denied these claims, and because of inconsistencies in McNamee's description of events – for example, in one statement he claimed he had been 'punched' whilst in a different statement he described the blow as a 'slap' – the CJC did not consider that there was sufficient evidence to refer the matter for consideration for disciplinary or criminal charges.

Noreen Jumbo, a key witness for the police, told the CJC a similar story, alleging that the police had coerced her into making a false statement that she had heard Kelvin saying he had 'damaged Patricia Carlton last night', and she only signed it because of police intimidation. She was then treated as a hostile witness, and wasn't called to give evidence after the preliminary hearing. Again the CJC did not support progressing the complaint for further action.

All four were making similar complaints about the police's

conduct when interviewing Condren and the witnesses. But, as we have seen, although the CJC produced a 136-page report addressing the various allegations, it ultimately found that no police officer should face either criminal or disciplinary charges.

EXPERT INSERT: FALSE CONFESSIONS

A confession is a written or oral statement in which a person admits to having committed a crime.

Many of the nation's wrongful convictions are based on false or coerced confessions, but you are probably wondering why someone would confess to a crime they have not committed. There are many factors that contribute to people making false/coerced confessions, and amongst those over-represented in the false confessor population are those suffering from psychiatric disorders, as well as individuals with intellectual disabilities who are more susceptible to suggestion, and minors or others highly influenced by the power of authority. In addition, confessions can be coerced, through false promises, threats, or intimidation.

Together, these fall into three types of false confessions; voluntary, compliant, and persuaded.

Voluntary false confessions commonly occur when an individual has underlying psychological or psychiatric problems. The confessor may be seeking notoriety or infamy, they may genuinely believe they are responsible for a crime and be seeking punishment or absolution, or they may not be able to differentiate reality from fantasy. Investigators are generally good at identifying this type of confessor.

A compliant false confession is where the suspect knowingly falsely confesses to escape the stressful situation, or to take advantage of a promise of leniency – these occur when the investigator uses stress, pressure, or coercion during the questioning process. Violence can also be used to elicit compliant (also known as coerced) confessions. Compliant confessions are normally withdrawn shortly afterwards.

A persuaded false confession, on the other hand, is when the questioning procedure leads the suspect to genuinely – but erroneously – believe that they were involved in the crime because they come to doubt their own memory of events.

The only requirement for a confession to be deemed admissible in court is that it was obtained voluntarily. However, procedural issues and laws brought in at a later time can affect the admissibility of a confession.

A case in point when considering false confessions is that of the abduction and murder of three-year-old Cheryl Grimmer from Fairy Meadow Beach, Wollongong, in January 1970. Eighteen months after Cheryl was taken, a 17-year-old boy confessed to the crime. The police did not take this confession seriously, deeming it false, and although they did not remove the person from their list of persons of interest in the case, he was not charged with any crimes at the time. In 2011 a coroner formally announced Cheryl was dead, even though her body has never been found, and simultaneously suggested New South Wales Police re-open the investigation into her disappearance. In 2016, 46 years after the child had been taken, as part of the case review, a detective from the New South Wales Police Cold Case Homicide Squad re-evaluated the boy's confession and decided there were too many accuracies within it to ignore. Following further investigations, in 2017 a 64-year-old man who was living in Melbourne was arrested and charged for Cheryl's abduction and murder – the same man that had confessed in 1971 (his identity is suppressed, as he was a minor at the time). However, in 2018 he pleaded not guilty and withdrew the confession he had made as a boy.

The Supreme Court was tasked with deciding if the confession should be used as evidence against the accused, however it was declared inadmissible on the grounds that at the time the confession was made, the 17-year-old did not have a parent, guardian, independent support person, or legal representative, as well as the fact that he was considered vulnerable – two psychiatrists gave evidence stating that he was below average intelligence and had had a difficult upbringing. Although there was no legal requirement on the police to provide guardianship for a minor during the time the interview was conducted, a law was later passed that required this, so the statute was applied retrospectively in this case; the judge was relying on the issue of substantive fairness as opposed to procedural fairness.

The Crown's case depended largely on the confession, and without a body or any forensic evidence, and now with a retracted confession, the case against the accused was dropped as the NSW Attorney General, Mark Speakman, was unwilling to instruct the Department of Public Prosecution to pursue it, as he did not think there was a reasonable chance of achieving a successful prosecution. In essence, that means we will probably never know if the confession was false or true, or ultimately who abducted and murdered Cheryl Grimmer, and the family may never get the closure they have desperately sought for almost 50 years.

'MR A': THE ALTERNATIVE SUSPECT

Mr A, or Andrew Christopher Albury as he was later identified, was a strong suspect in Patricia's murder – he was a sadistic serial killer, who at the time of his confession to killing an Aboriginal woman in Mount Isa, was on trial for murder in Darwin. We don't know exactly how many people he killed, but he has admitted to 13 murders. However, it should be noted that the Northern Territory Supreme Court (in *The Queen v Albury* [2004] NTSC 59) stated that an investigation concluded the confessions to the additional 11 were fictional, so we will never really know how many murders Albury was guilty of.

But we do know that Albury had known details of Patricia's murder that only the perpetrator could have been aware of. So, in all likelihood, Patricia was one of Andrew Albury's victims.

Regardless of how good a fit Albury was, to the great surprise of investigators and the NT prosecutors, Mount Isa police declined an invitation to attend Albury's trial in Darwin in November 1983, although it is clear this should have been an important part of their investigation.

So, police had all but dismissed Albury's confession. As far as they were concerned they had their man: Kelvin Condren. And he was found guilty, case closed.

That is until the investigative journalists from *Page One* started to re-evaluate the evidence against Kelvin. They accessed the confession Albury made in jail, and came to the conclusion that it matched the attack on Patricia in key details. The police had not verified Albury's movements, but the *Page One* team did – he was in Mount Isa on the night of the murder. They went further, talking to people in town who may have had information, and eventually, through good, old-fashioned investigative footwork, tracked down Price and Millican. The journalists knew they had struck gold – independent, credible, reliable witnesses with no personal connection to the accused or the victim. No reason to lie.

This was clearly a huge breakthrough, but one the police should have made had they done their jobs properly. They should have canvassed the local area, as the journalists did, and interviewed the local shopkeepers and other potential witnesses. Foundations of a police investigation. The police should also have attended Albury's murder trial.

But instead, they had suffered from tunnel vision or confirmation bias.

They had their man and that was it, job done.

Except, as we know now, it wasn't.

Born in Victoria, Albury first came to the attention of police when he murdered 29-year-old Gloria Pindan, an Aboriginal woman, with a broken bottle in Darwin on 25 November 1983. This was no straightforward attack – Gloria had been found in a flower bed of a vacant lot, with her dress pulled up over her head and her knickers torn and around her left ankle. Albury had stabbed Gloria many times, leaving her with 28 external injuries. He had cut off her nipples and gouged out one of her eyes before throwing it into the grass four metres away from where he killed her. The attack had been so brutal that blood spatter could be seen one metre up a nearby wall.

This had been a blitz-style attack, and Gloria had not even had the chance to protect herself, as there were no defence injuries. No single injury was the cause of death, instead the pathologist determined that multiple injuries were the accumulative cause.

Albury was just 22 years old and already an extremely violent and dangerous man. He was easily caught after the attack on Gloria – his shirt had been covered in blood, so he took it off and discarded it in a nearby bin. On discovering Gloria's body, the police soon also discovered the shirt – a white silk cowboy shirt.

The day after the murder, after some initial inquires looking for a man wearing a shirt fitting that description, they received intelligence that a person of interest had been drinking in a local hotel the night before.

Within two hours of the body being discovered, the police had their man. Albury had gone back to the pub he'd been in the night before. Albury was an alcoholic and didn't remember much about Gloria's murder or taking off his shirt and throwing it away. But when the police caught up with him, he still had dried blood behind his ear from when he had killed her.

He was taken back to the police station for questioning, and soon confessed. He had only arrived in Darwin the night before he killed Gloria, as he was taking a break from his role as a contract shooter of feral animals.

Albury gave no real motive; he just enjoyed killing.

He said that when he was killing animals he didn't get the urge to kill anyone, but when he was on holiday from his job, he 'had to kill something'.

When asked why he removed Gloria's eye, he simply answered, 'No reason, I enjoyed the killing'.

It's just that simple for a man like Albury. And just that heartbreaking: Gloria was just in the wrong place at the wrong time. This was an opportunistic murder by a sadistic serial killer.

And solid police work quickly saw him in custody. If he'd left town, it would have been extremely hard for the police to track down Gloria's killer, as random opportunistic attacks often leave little for police to go on. If only the police had acted so swiftly and professionally following Patricia's murder.

Albury admitted that part of his victim selection was racist – he told the detectives that he hated Aboriginal people, and believed in the ideals of the Ku Klux Klan. He also admitted to assaulting

Aboriginal people before, telling a psychiatrist after his arrest that when he was younger he and his friends used to attack them with sticks.

He was totally blasé about the violence he'd employed, showed no emotion, and was not fazed by being questioned by police over such a serious crime. He showed no nervousness at all.

This man was a true, cold-blooded killer, with no empathy for his victims who would have kept on killing if he had not been caught.

And it was clear that this was not his first murder. He claimed to have killed his first person at age 15, and given he is clearly a violent psychopath, this would not surprise me.

His first victim was allegedly a 14-year-old boy, who he murdered and then buried under a boat shed on the Mornington Peninsula.

He also claimed he was one of 'The Family' murderers – the name given to a group of men believed responsible for the kidnapping, sexual abuse, torture, and murder of five teenagers around Adelaide, between 1979 and 1983. Victims included 16-year-old Alan Barnes, 25-year-old Neil Muir, 14-year-old Peter Stogneff, 18-year-old Mark Langley, and 15-year-old Richard Kelvin. Four of the five murders are unsolved, and only one man, Bevan Spencer von Einem, has ever been brought to justice, for the murder of Richard Kelvin.

Other claims Albury has made are that he murdered a man with a machete before throwing his body into the Port Adelaide River, and that he killed Alfred Beales, a sleeping pensioner, by stomping him to death in the dry Todd River bed in Alice Springs. He also said that he poisoned alcohol to murder three Aboriginal people at the same river bed in 1981.

In July 1984, Albury was found guilty of Gloria's murder, and was initially sentenced to life without the possibility of parole. However, in 2001 changes to legislation in Queensland put an end to indefinite sentences for murder, and Albury's sentence was changed to a default 20 years without parole. At this time he had served 18 years.

The Director of Public Prosecutions (DPP), Rex Wild QC, applied to the Northern Territory Supreme Court, petitioning for Albury to remain in prison for the rest of his life. Chief Justice Brian Martin (Chief Justice of the Supreme Court in the NT) was the man who had to make the decision, and to assist him he was provided with many psychiatric reports, which all agreed on one point – Albury was a very dangerous man.

The application to keep him in prison without the possibility of parole was granted in November 2004, almost 21 years after he killed Gloria.

In September 2016 he was called to give evidence into a Coronial inquest into the disappearance of 20-year-old Tony Jones, who was last seen in Townsville in November 1982. The last contact Tony had had with his family was when he phoned them to tell them he was planning to hitchhike from Townsville to Mount Isa. Tony then vanished, and over 37 years later, his whereabouts remains a mystery. Albury was dialled into the court from Darwin, but he refused to cooperate, saying only that 'Jones will stay where I planted him'.

Before he hung up, however, he was asked again about Patricia Carlton, and re-confessed to her murder.

Police from across Australia have investigated Albury's claims, including officers from Townsville in 2014 who went to speak to Albury about various ongoing cases, at which time he claimed to have murdered up to 14 hitchhikers on a spree as he moved between Townsville and Mount Isa between 1970 and 1982. Police have investigated these claims, and have discounted many, however they believe he is responsible for a number of other cold case murders.

After his arrest for killing Gloria in 1983, Albury was formally diagnosed as schizophrenic, which would have resulted in delusions and hallucinations, so he has not been tried for the additional crimes.

There is no doubt in my mind that there are other victims. In a letter to Chief Justice Brian Martin he said, 'I will kill again, it's what I do for an occupation'. And in a letter to prison authorities he wrote in 2004, Albury claimed his 'chance of reoffending in violent murderous manner is 100 per cent (hopefully soon)'.

And he was true to his word. He didn't stop in prison. In 1988, whilst he was housed at Darwin Correctional Centre, the prison attempted to reintegrate Albury back into the inmate community. It didn't work; he attacked a fellow inmate with a cricket bat.

In 1989 he was charged with attempted murder, but was acquitted on the grounds of insanity as he claimed voices in his head told him to do it; this came to light during an interview with a psychiatrist, and led to the diagnosis of schizophrenia.

But he was not psychotic.

The psychiatrist confirmed Albury was a very dangerous man who 'still fantasises about killing people . . . there is also a sadistic element to his killing. He derives pleasure from the mutilation of the body of the victim'.

What became clear is that Albury is such a damaged individual, he can be described as one of Australia's most pathological and dangerous killers.

THE IMPLICATIONS

The Condren case marks a landmark situation in Queensland criminal justice. For Kelvin to be convicted of murder, have one appeal dismissed, to wait in jail for over six years only to have his conviction quashed, then to be exonerated and be awarded $400,000 as an ex gratia compensation payment is extraordinary.

A win for justice?

Well, no.

The concern is that he was convicted in the first place, and that comes down to a number of things.

This case represents the total failure of the criminal justice system to do its job – it failed Kelvin Condren, Patricia Carlton and the entire community.

Racism was evident at every level of this crime – from Albury's selection of Patricia as a victim due to her Aboriginality, and throughout Kelvin's conviction – from the police, to the courts, and the wider community. Even the CJC isn't above criticism, as in 1992 it published a response to the claims entitled *Report on the Investigation into the Complaints of Kelvin Ronald Condren and Others*.

In the report the CJC concluded that no one should be subject to disciplinary or criminal action as a result of the miscarriage of justice Kelvin suffered – a man lost over six years of his life, and individuals were clearly to blame for their actions, yet they were not asked to take responsibility for them.

More damning of the CJC's assessment of the police's failure to adequately canvas the local neighbourhood for witnesses, it stated that 'In the Commission's view, it is not clear that further reliable information about Ms Carlton's movements on the night in question could have been obtained by further investigations by police'.

This is clearly at odds with what a top investigative journalist managed to unearth with a little effort.

Within just a few years of Condren's successful appeal, the Royal Commission into Aboriginal Deaths in Custody (RCIADIC, 1987–1991) was established to explore the complex relationship between race and the criminal justice system in Australia, and to determine why so many Aboriginal people were in prison.

The Royal Commission examined and identified a number of elements that combine to illuminate the contemporary disadvantages (social, cultural, economic, and legal) that many Aboriginal and Torres Strait Islander peoples in Australia experience. Included were deaths in custody that were the result of suicide, natural causes, medical conditions, or injuries sustained as a result of police action between 1 January 1980 and 31 May 1989. This totalled 99 deaths.

It provided 339 recommendations to reduce Aboriginal deaths in custody. Very few have been implemented.

Although the Royal Commission did not conclude that the 99 deaths were due to police violence, it concluded by saying that 'glaring deficiencies existed in the standard of care afforded to many of the deceased'.

The report found that Aboriginal people did not die at higher numbers in custody than non-Aboriginal people.

But, and it's a big but, the report also stated that:

> The conclusions are clear. Aboriginal people die in custody at a rate relative to their proportion of the whole population, which is totally unacceptable and which would not be tolerated if it occurred in the non-Aboriginal community. But this occurs not because Aboriginal people in custody are more likely to die than others in custody, but because the Aboriginal population is grossly over represented in custody. Too many Aboriginal people are in custody too often.

Including Kelvin Condren for six years.

THE OVER-REPRESENTATION OF ABORIGINAL AND TORRES STRAIT ISLANDER PEOPLE IN PRISON

Aboriginal and Torres Strait Islander people are overrepresented compared to non-Indigenous people at all levels of the criminal justice system – from juvenile institutions, to those being held in prison cells, to adult prisons.

ATSI people make up 28 per cent of the total adult prison population, even though they comprise only around two per cent of the overall Australian population. The state-by-state rates vary significantly, with the Northern Territory (85 per cent) and Western Australia (38 per cent) having the highest rates of Indigenous prisoners. The picture is particularly bleak for young Indigenous people, who comprise 54 per cent of those in youth detention across Australia, but make up only seven per cent of the general youth population. The problem is worse in the NT, where 97 per cent of young people in detention are Aboriginal.

And it's actually getting worse, not better; since 2004, the number of Aboriginal Australians in custody has gone up by 88 per cent, compared to a 28 per cent increase for people who aren't Aboriginal.

There are many reasons for this, including social and economic circumstances, and the links to ongoing contemporary experiences, as well as those to previous generations' experiences of colonisation.

The ongoing impacts of colonisation have led to contemporary inequalities across many areas for Indigenous people, including poor housing, low standards of health and high mortality rates. Unemployment rates are also high, and wages low when compared to the rest of the population. This leads to endemic poverty and ultimately increased contact with the criminal justice system.

We also know that Aboriginal people are over-represented in terms of wrongful convictions.

As we have seen, wrongful convictions occur for a number of reasons – one of which is false confessions. The problems can be compounded for Indigenous people by translation and language difficulties, insensitive or wholly inadequate defence representation, pressures to plead guilty, as well as racist stereotypes that associate

Aboriginal people with criminal activity. This systemic discrimination has at times led prosecutors to be willing to progress weak cases, and juries to be willing to find accused persons guilty when there is very little evidence that culpability exists.

Such was the situation with Kelvin Condren, who can be seen to have been subject to a number of factors that can lead to innocent people going to prison.

And rarely are they compensated for their losses. Though impossible to quantify, when the justice system has let them down so badly, surely some dispensation should be available.

Kelvin was, in this sense 'lucky'; he was awarded $400,000 as an ex gratia or 'act of grace' payment in 1995 by the Queensland Government.

Others in similar situations don't even get this.

In 1991 in Western Australia, Jeanie Angel was exonerated for the wilful murder of her neighbour, after having spent two years in prison. Like Kelvin, Jeanie had allegedly made a confession to police. And like in Kelvin's case, other witnesses had told the police they had seen the deceased victim with other women from the community, but the police failed to pursue these lines of inquiry.

Jeanie claimed later, however, that the confession was coerced through violence, in that she stated that she was physically assaulted before signing the confession. Two other women later confessed to the murder, the same women named in the witness statements as having been with the victim, and Jeanie's conviction was quashed on appeal on the grounds that it was unsafe. Unlike Condren, however, Jeanie was never awarded compensation to help mitigate against her lost two years whilst she was incarcerated, with the Attorney General of WA, Joseph Berinson QC, rejecting her request, and a representative clarified the position by saying that 'an act of grace payment is made only in the most exceptional circumstances, and this is not such a case'. Apparently, the police's mishandling of the case, and alleged abuse and coercion of a confession, and a woman losing two years of her life in prison did not constitute 'exceptional' circumstances. Worrying.

Equalling troubling is the link between political will and media influence – those individuals most likely to be awarded compensation are the ones with media backing, or significant public interest. If you don't have that, you have little chance of receiving any remuneration.

Although the RCIADIC delivered its findings in 1991, the same problems and patterns of over-incarceration still exist. Various policies have been put in place to tackle this issue, however dominant social attitudes can negatively impact the outcomes of policy responses, which allows biases to remain.

For example, the misconception that Indigenous youths are delinquents leads to over-policing, and therefore higher rates of young Aboriginal and Torres Strait Islander people being held on remand and being prosecuted.

A key factor that plays into these disproportionately high rates is having one/both parents incarcerated, as research and anecdotal evidence suggests that incarceration has intergenerational impacts. Separation of parents from their children and broader communities can lead to mental health issues for both parents and children. For children who visit family members who are incarcerated, this can lead to normalisation of the situation, reducing the intended deterrent effect. We also know that strong family ties and support post-release reduces recidivism (repeat offending). When relationships break down because people are in prison – sometimes at great distances from their loved ones – this increases the chances of the prisoner offending again in the future.

An example of the injustice in the criminal 'justice' system for Indigenous people is the use of fines. This is particularly impacting ATSI women, who are over 21 times more likely to end up in prison than non-Indigenous females, higher than for non-ATSI men. Jurisdictionally, WA has the highest female ATSI imprisonment rate, which is having a significant detrimental effect on families. This hit the headlines in 2019 when news broke of an ATSI mother of five who was arrested on an outstanding warrant for unpaid fines when she contacted the police regarding a family violence complaint. The ramifications are obvious – seek protection from the police when you find yourself the victim of family violence, and risk arrest for unpaid fines. Under those circumstances, many mothers would choose to stay in a dangerous home environment than risk being sent to prison and therefore being separated from their children.

It is a terrible catch-22. Western Australia is the only state that regularly jails people for unpaid fines, and the majority of those sent to prison for this are Aboriginal women; for every $250 owed, the offender spends one day in prison. Most of those jailed for this offence are unemployed with no capacity to pay, so instead they are taken away from their families. Injustice piled on injustice.

Restorative justice practices are one way of helping to reduce the high rates of Indigenous incarceration. These include youth conferencing, circle sentencing, and Aboriginal courts. There has been some success with these methods, but they cannot stand alone. There also needs to be improvement in health and social services, as well as specialised legal services that provide Indigenous people with representation when required. More services are needed to advise on divertive measures, to provide rehabilitative facilities for drug and alcohol dependency and improved assistance for those suffering from family violence.

We clearly still have a very long way to go.

IN THE END . . .

A young man lost over six years of his life for a crime he did not commit, and a man who is likely guilty will never be prosecuted on the grounds that he is mentally unfit. I am not sure this will bring much solace to Patricia's family.

Research shows us that Aboriginal and Torres Strait Islander people are over-represented in the criminal justice system – it is a pervasive problem, and one we don't seem to be able to address.

This miscarriage of justice occurred because of endemic racism, and was solved because the media asked questions that the police should have asked. Had the media not got involved, an innocent man would have remained in jail for life. In this way, the media can have oversight over the criminal justice system, keeping it honest, and helping to set right some of the wrongs.

THREE

ANDREW MALLARD:
WHEN PROSECUTION BECAME PERSECUTION
(1994)

'I know what they did to me and it's the truth. They framed
me for a murder I did not commit.'

Andrew Mallard, speaking to ABC's *Australian Story* in 2010

Perth, capital and largest city of Western Australia, was established
where the Swan River meets the coast. The city is a sparkling jewel
on Australia's west coast. With a population of 1.2 million, by the
1990s Australia's sunniest capital city had blossomed into a vibrant
business and cultural hub, with over 70 per cent of WA's residents
choosing to live within the city limits. Young people were drawn to
Perth and there was a trendy café scene and unassuming suburban
neighbourhoods to raise families.

But this was not a utopia. In the mid to late 1990s, WA had the
highest rates for some property crimes, including unlawful entry
with intent as well as motor vehicle theft. In the mid-1990s, assault
rates were also high, with WA having the third highest number
behind the NT and SA. The state also held the highest number of
sexual assaults anywhere in Australia.

Mosman Park is a suburb west of the city, located on the banks of the Swan River and bounded by the Indian Ocean to the west. A wealthy suburb, boasting some of the most expensive real estate in Australia, this is somewhere a boutique business should thrive, and its owner be safe. However, the City of Light went dark and this illusion of security shattered in 1995 when businesswoman Pamela Lawrence was violently murdered in her jewellery store.

I know Perth well, and one of my favourite spots in Australia is Kings Park, as I love overlooking the iridescent Swan Rover and sparkling white buildings of Perth's CBD. I found myself doing just that in December 2019 on a business trip to the city. But in addition to seeing the beauty, I also wanted to get a sense of the scene of Pamela's brutal murder. To visit Mosman Park, to see the area through the eyes of the man who had killed Pamela. The scene of a murder and the beginning of a miscarriage of justice.

I have included this case as it asks some serious questions of our criminal justice system and the right to the presumption of innocence, which we all assume we will benefit from should we ever be accused of a crime. However, this was not a luxury afforded to Andrew Mallard, who was found guilty of Pamela's murder. Mallard spent over 12 years in prison. He had no history of violence and no weapon linking him to the crime was ever found. He was just a vulnerable man in the wrong place at the wrong time. And easy pickings for lazy policemen. Andrew was eventually released, but only because a politician and a journalist went to extraordinary lengths to set the record straight.

This miscarriage of justice made the news again in April 2019 when Mallard, then 56, was killed in a hit-and-run car crash in Los Angeles whilst on a visit to his fiancée from his new home in Britain, where he had moved in 2006 after being exonerated.

He only had 13 years of freedom after his release – a timely reminder that convicted does not equal guilty, and why we need people brave enough to ask the tough questions and search for the confronting answers so that things can change for the better.

THE CASE

On Monday 23 May 1994, wife and mother Pamela Suzanne Lawrence was brutally bludgeoned in broad daylight whilst working at her jewellery shop, Flora Metallica, on Glyde Street in Mosman Park, Perth.

Pamela not only owned and ran the shop, but also made the jewellery herself, in a small shed out the back where she spent most of her day working. An assistant, Mrs Jacqueline Barsden, also worked there and was working the day Pamela was killed.

On the day of her death, Pamela went shopping, returning around 2pm, before going down to her workshop around 2:10pm. Mrs Barsden didn't see Pamela again that day, as she left at her normal time of 3pm, locking the door of the now unattended shop so that it could only be opened from the outside with a key, but could still be opened from inside.

Mrs Barsden had a 13-year-old daughter, Katherine, and around 4:20pm Jacqueline called her mother, Mrs Wood, to ask if she could pick Katherine up from St Hilda's Girls School, where she was a pupil. Katherine would later prove to be a key Crown witness.

At around 6pm Pamela was found on the floor of the shop, face down in a pool of blood. She had suffered several head injuries, severe enough that her skull was fractured in three separate places. There were three distinct groups of injuries, one to the right front side of her head involving her temple, a second to the left covering the forehead and temple, and a third group on the back of her head. The pathologist determined that the injuries were caused by a blunt object that had been used to inflict a number of blows to each region. The murder weapon was never found, and in fact the pathologist was unable to determine what type of weapon exactly caused the injuries sustained.

The blood pattern evidence indicated that she had been attacked in the shop, and that she was lying on the floor when she obtained some of her injuries. She was then dragged to the rear of the shop, where more blows were inflicted.

By 6:15pm Pamela's husband had become worried that she had not returned home from work, so he phoned the shop but there was no answer and the answering machine had not been switched on. Becoming more concerned, he drove the two-minute journey to the shop to check on Pamela. When he arrived the lights were still on, and the 'open' sign was still hanging on the door.

The front door was locked so he needed his key to get in. Once inside, he noticed some blood on a partition, and heard a groan coming from the back of the shop. Rushing towards the sound, he found his wife lying on the floor, with blood around her mouth and making gurgling sounds. He put her in the recovery position and called 000. This call was registered as taking place at 6:37pm.

The ambulance arrived at 6:45pm, by which point the police were already on scene, having got to the shop at 6:42pm. Whilst the crew attended to his wife, he checked the rest of the shop. He found the back door closed but unlocked, and the door to the workshop at the back open and the lights still on. The copper bath, which Pamela used to plate jewellery, was still switched on.

Mr Lawrence then went back to the main shop to determine if anything had been taken. No jewellery was missing, and the cash was still in the cashbox under the counter. Pamela's handbag was on a shelf in the shop, and her purse and credit cards had been taken. Mr Lawrence said that his wife normally kept between $100–$150 cash in her purse. Mr Lawrence also thought an expanding spanner, which Pamela used in her work, was missing from the workshop, but he could not be certain. The tool in question was 25 centimetres long, and could also be described as a wrench.

Pamela was taken to hospital, but died as a result of her injuries a few hours later.

This violent crime sparked a manhunt, but initially the police didn't have a main suspect, and had to narrow down a list of around 664 possibilities. After some initial investigations, they created a shortlist of 136 persons of interest.

Andrew Mallard was on the list because he had come to the attention of the police previously. Andrew had been living on the streets following a nervous breakdown, and was arrested when he attempted a burglary dressed as a police officer. Instead of going to prison, as is the case with others who have been charged with a crime but deemed too unwell to plead, he was placed at Graylands Psychiatric Hospital in Perth – a facility deemed outdated in 2014 as it was modelled on the old-fashioned asylums.

Mallard was interviewed by police several times over six days whilst still a patient at Graylands. On 26 May, Detectives David Caporn and Mark Emmett spoke to Andrew about his movements on the day Pamela was killed. He told them he had caught a taxi that evening and walked past the shop and seen the police activity about 7pm. Having seen the police activity, he assumed there had been a burglary.

The police came back to speak to Mallard again the next day, as they wanted to iron out some inconsistencies between his story and what the taxi driver who had dropped Andrew off, Mr Peverall, had told them later after they had tracked him down.

Andrew asked if it mattered, and they replied that it did, as Pamela had been murdered and he didn't have an alibi. At this point they confirmed he was a suspect in her death, and he provided additional information as to his movements, which largely revolved around his attempts to source marijuana.

On 30 May Caporn and Emmett interviewed Mallard again at Graylands, and this time removed items of his clothing for analysis – as whoever killed Pamela would inevitably have been covered in blood spatter as a result of the traumatic nature of her injuries.

His clothes were tested, but none of Pamela's blood was found on his clothing.

On the morning of 10 June 1994 Mallard was released from Graylands to answer a charge at court in Perth. That same day he was taken from court to a police station. He was then interviewed over the course of eight hours and 20 minutes, with seven breaks, in relation to the attack on Pamela.

At no point was he cautioned or charged before or during the interview.

The interview went for a very long time and only a very small amount was recorded. The format was that one officer asked questions, whilst the other took detailed, handwritten notes.

Over the course of this very protracted interview, Andrew gave various accounts of his movements, admitting to having been at the jewellers and then denying it.

Altogether, it was a very confused, and confusing, conversation. The whole process would have been exhausting and intimidating for Andrew, who remember had just been released from a psychiatric facility and was already in a vulnerable state.

This distress was apparent when Andrew became upset during questioning. He began to cry and made comments like 'there are a lot of blanks'.

Regardless of the vulnerable nature of the suspect, as well as Mallard's obvious fatigue and distress, the officers persevered with the interview.

Andrew then gave a detailed account of surprising Pamela in the shop when he was casing it whilst planning to burgle it, and that he had hit her because he was scared of being caught.

During the interview, Andrew hypothesised how Pamela might have been attacked, and drew pictures to support his story. He even provided a drawing of the weapon that could have been used to inflict her head injuries – a wrench.

Mallard also helped the police explain why they didn't find any blood on his clothing, saying at interview that he had been covered in blood, but that he had 'washed them in salt water because salt water fucks with forensics'. He claimed to have done this by the river.

The police took this to be a confession, although he never signed it, and charged Andrew with the murder, as they said his confession, together with the rough sketch of the weapon, included information only the killer could have known.

Chapter two looked at the case of Kelvin Condren, whose alleged confession led to his subsequent arrest and imprisonment. We can see clear parallels here. False confessions are one of the main factors that lead to miscarriages of justice.

Like Kelvin, Andrew was vulnerable and could have made a false confession under any one of the categories I outlined: voluntary, if he genuinely believed he was responsible for Pamela's murder, compliant, as he was under considerable psychological stress during the police questioning, or persuaded, if he began to doubt his own memory of events. So although his confession may have been given freely, it could hardly be classed as reliable.

His statement also contradicted evidence by the pathologist, Dr Cooke, who stated in his report that the wrench in Mallard's drawing could not have caused all of the injuries, as whilst they were consistent with a blunt instrument having been used, other injuries of Pamela's were inflicted by a weapon that had a chopping or blade type surface as well, which Mallard's drawing did not depict.

And Cooke had tested the theory. Having sourced a wrench similar to the one Andrew had drawn, he conducted trauma tests on a pig's skull to see if he could replicate the injuries inflicted to Pamela's skull. He could not.

This was a reliable indicator that the tool Andrew drew did not cause those injuries.

Animal studies of this nature are not unusual in forensic science. It is, of course, best to test forensic theories on artefacts as closely related to the original as possible, but when it comes to trauma studies, this can be difficult. There are strict ethical limitations on what can be done to human remains, even those that have been specifically bequeathed to programs for forensic research (such as those at the Australian Facility for Taphonomic Research, run by the University of Technology Sydney, where I undertake human decomposition studies). As a result, researchers and clinicians often use pigs as proxies for humans when attempting to test a theory, as they are the closest mammal in size and shape to adult humans.

But the police didn't care about the truth. And they weren't finished with Andrew.

On 17 June two new detectives, Brandham and Carter, interviewed Mallard. During this procedure, he gave a detailed confession regarding how he killed Pamela, in the first person, although some of the statements he made did not fit with what the police knew had happened.

This interview was conducted even though the interviewers should have known that Mallard had been out the previous evening at a nightclub and was sleep-deprived, and had also been beaten.

The last 20 minutes of the three-hour interview were videoed – 20 minutes of a total of 11 hours of interviews – but was not like a normal videotaped confession where the suspect provides information. Rather, the detectives asked leading questions about what Mallard had previously said, to which Mallard simply confirmed that what was being suggested was correct. As an example:

Detective: You told us that you went out front on Glyde Street and that you were looking back and you saw that the Flora Metallica – the door was shut?

Mallard: Yes.

Detective: And that you thought it was closed so it was safe to do a break. Is that what you told us?

Mallard: That's correct.

Later Andrew would state that he made these comments after he was fed the information directly by the officers interviewing him. This is supported by some of the responses taken directly from Andrew's statements, in which he flips from first to third person when describing what happened to Pamela.

When asked the question, 'What did he hit her with?' Mallard responded, 'A wrench. *He* couldn't let her tell anybody. *He* was scared.'

And again, when asked how many times he hit her, he responded, 'I don't know, a lot. *He* can't get caught.'

It appears the police had been feeding Andrew information from the scene to make it look as if he had guilty knowledge, or what is known as '*actus reus*'.

EXPERT INSERT: THE BASIC COMPONENTS OF AN OFFENCE

A criminal offence comprises two components, *mens rea* (the mental element) and *actus reus* (the physical or conduct element). The prosecution is generally required to prove these components and the elements making up a criminal offence to a standard beyond reasonable doubt (the legal standard in Australia and many other common-law based systems, such as England).

Mens rea is a Latin phrase which means 'guilty mind'. In a criminal case, it is generally necessary to prove that an accused person has the intention to commit a crime or that by not acting a crime will be committed. For someone to be found guilty by a court of a crime, the prosecution must usually demonstrate that *mens rea* was present.

The *actus reus* is sometimes referred to as the physical or conduct element of a crime, as it largely relates to the conduct of the suspect. In addition to showing *mens rea* was present, for an accused to be found criminally culpable the prosecution must show that the person committed the guilty act.

Whilst motive is not necessary to prove that a crime has been committed, it can be of importance for jurors in a criminal trial to understand why an accused may have acted in a particular way. There is no requirement that the prosecution show that the accused's actions were premeditated with some crimes being committed opportunistically or with reckless indifference to human life.

There is a legal presumption that an accused is mentally fit to stand trial on a criminal charge. An accused must be able to understand at the time of the trial the nature of the criminal charge and criminal proceedings and to be able to instruct a lawyer. Should an accused have a cognitive or mental health impairment that impacts on their understanding, then the court may need to consider whether the person is fit to stand trial. A defence of mental illness or mental impairment may also be raised if the accused was mentally ill at the time of the criminal offence. An accused can be subject to treatment or detention in a mental health facility should they be unable to stand trial on a criminal charge or are found not guilty of a crime on the basis of being mentally ill.

Shaun McCarthy, Director,
University of Newcastle Legal Centre

There were more problems with this videotaped interview. It appears that prior to it being recorded, Andrew may have been shown crime scene images of the deceased. He began one of his answers, when asked about the attack on Pamela, with 'Well, judging from the photographs . . .'. At trial and again at the appeal, Mallard stated that the police showed him just one photograph, where the victim was lying in a prone (chest down) position. The detectives denied ever showing him this image. If Mallard was telling the truth here, it would explain how he could describe in accurate detail the injuries Pamela sustained.

The 'confession' was crucial to the Crown's case at trial, and as there was no forensic evidence linking Mallard to the murder, the prosecution relied on circumstantial information to help build its case against him. Andrew was in the area at the time of the attack, as he had been placed in police lock-up in East Perth at around 2:40pm on the day Pamela was killed, after being arrested for a break-and-enter and theft, and was released about an hour later. Andrew then caught a taxi in Perth between 4pm and 4:10pm, and was taken to Bel Air Flats at 2 Murray Avenue, Mosman Park – a 10-minute walk from Pamela's jewellery shop – arriving sometime between 4:45pm and 5pm. The taxi driver could not be more precise about the time. Mallard told the taxi driver he was going into the flats and then coming back to pay his fare, but he absconded.

Several other Crown witnesses gave evidence suggesting Mallard was around Murray Avenue around 5pm, including a Mrs Raine, who said she saw a man fitting Andrew's description on the ground floor of Bel Air Flats on 23 May between 5:15pm and 5:25pm. Raine said the man she saw was carrying an iron bar and a carton of chocolate milk. This does not match with other evidence, as the police records showed that Mallard had only $2 on him when he was taken into custody earlier in the day, and no iron bar, obviously.

No evidence was led as to where he supposedly got the bar, or why he had it.

Mrs Raine says she was sure she saw the same man again the following day, when Mallard was being arrested by the police on Murray Street. She later identified Andrew from a photo board as the man she'd seen at the flats on 23 May.

Katherine, the shop assistant Jacqueline Barsden's daughter, also gave eyewitness evidence. As arranged, her grandmother, Mrs Wood, had collected her from school. She remembered noticing the digital clock in the car reading 5pm, and a couple of minutes later they pulled up at a red traffic light opposite Flora Metallica. Katherine said during the trial that she saw a man standing in the shop, and that he caught her attention because he wasn't standing where a customer would wait, but behind a display area where only staff would go. So she made a mental note of his appearance, as his behaviour also struck her as strange. She described the man as '30–35 years old, medium build, slight beard, orange strawberry blond colour, scarf on his head, rustic orange border, slight pattern blue or green . . . I kept staring and I felt the moment that he saw me or we made eye contact, he bobbed down and I kept looking for another 30 seconds and he didn't appear. In those 30 seconds the lights changed to green and the car moved off. I didn't see Mrs Lawrence'. She also said the man was around six feet tall.

When she got home, Katherine made several crude drawings of the man she had seen in the shop, which she also annotated with important details, when trying to explain to her mother. She described a man with a slight beard but no moustache, with a scarf on his head that was a 'rustic orange colour', with additions of a slight green and blue pattern.

This was clearly important evidence, as the Crown would suggest that this man – who was clearly behaving suspiciously by dropping out of sight (we can assume to avoid being seen) and who the girl could describe in reasonable detail – was also the man who had killed Pamela.

Mrs Wood confirmed the girl's statement, both to the time she picked her up from school, and that when they were at the lights Katherine had said 'there's someone in mummy's shop'.

Normally it is not unusual for someone to be in a shop, but the girl felt the need to comment, suggesting that something about the scenario had jarred as strange to her. She was only 13 at the time of the incident, and 15 when she gave evidence in court, but clearly she was an astute teenager and an important witness.

Mallard gave evidence confirming he was in the shop, and that he had locked eyes with someone when a car was waiting at the traffic lights opposite. This placed Andrew, at his own admission, in the shop at around 5pm, demonstrating he had the opportunity to kill Pamela. He was also known to wear a velour cap sometimes, which was reddish in colour with a small pattern in shades of brown, and with an orange braid border. The cap, and whether Mallard was wearing it that day, would become important later.

Andrew had 'corroborated' Katherine's statement, apparently telling the police he had 'locked eyes' with a witness in a green car, then retracted this statement. The reliability of this comment was later discredited by an ophthalmologist, who examined Andrew and said his eye sight was so bad he couldn't have 'locked eyes' with anyone over such a distance. So if Andrew could not have made direct eye contact with Katherine in the car, he would not have ducked behind the counter to avoid being seen. He must have got the information provided by Katherine about the person's behaviour in the shop from somewhere, and realistically only the police could have told him, again indicating that his confession was false.

We know that Pamela was alive and well at 5:10pm, as a further witness, Barry Whitford, stated that a woman (who can only have been Pamela) called from Flora Metallica to discuss some products. This call occurred at 5:10pm, confirmed by Telecom.

Mallard offered an alibi, but it was a weak one easily challenged by the prosecution. He said that after he got out of the taxi, which he freely admitted was him as suggested by the witness, he went to flat 3/10 Murray Avenue at about 5:30pm, where a Michelle Engelhardt lived, and with whom Mallard had shared a flat for a while.

He changed his clothes because he was wet as it had been raining; in fact a big freak storm had struck that day, so he was drenched. He only spent about a minute at the flat, after which he said he was walking around knocking on several doors in an attempt to obtain marijuana, but got no answer.

Engelhardt gave evidence to suggest he did not arrive until 6:30pm and stayed until 7pm, however, as Mallard was known to have been on a train from Mosman Park to Fremantle at 6:58pm, we know her timings are inaccurate. Even if she was wrong about the time he left, she may have been more reliable with his arrival time of around 6:30pm, which would mean he was not at the flat at the time Pamela was attacked.

A number of witnesses at the flats gave evidence that they had seen Mallard going door-to-door looking to buy drugs the day before, on Sunday 22 May, so it was suggested in court that he may have got his days confused, or may be lying to give himself an alibi for the time Pamela was attacked. If the jury rejected his alibi, it meant Mallard could not account for where he was at the crucial time, giving him the opportunity to have been at the jewellery shop around 5pm.

Engelhardt made several statements to police about Mallard's movements the day Pamela was killed. In a handwritten draft statement, when talking about the time she got home at around 3pm until she says Andrew arrived at 6:30pm, the following appears:

'[Mallard's] hat was hanging above the door inside' (where it was commonly kept when he wasn't wearing it) followed by 'He didn't have any sought [sic] of headwear on.'

However, when the statement was typed up, the comment about the hat being at the flat was missing, as was all reference to his hair being wet, and the line about him not having any headwear on was replaced with, 'I'm not sure of what trousers he had on or if he was wearing his cap. It was raining and he was wet.' At trial she gave evidence that Andrew had gone straight to the bathroom when he came in, and emerged drying his hair due to the rain – which further indicates his head was uncovered when he had been outside, otherwise his hair would have been protected from the rain.

Perhaps most significantly, the handwritten draft statement was not made available to the defence, therefore at trial they were not aware of the significant discrepancy between the handwritten and typed versions. This would form one of the grounds of appeal later, as they did not have the chance to cross-examine Engelhardt on this key aspect of her evidence.

EXPERT INSERT: RULES OF DISCLOSURE

A prosecutor has special duties to see that justice is done and not to act as a pure adversary. The professional obligations of a prosecutor in Australia are no different from those imposed on every prosecutor or prosecuting authority in the common law system. Prosecutors' ethical and professional duties can be sourced from the three basic principles of fairness, independence, and impartiality. These are all aspects of the rule of law and underpin the right to a fair trial.

Fairness – Prosecutors must act fairly at all times (pre-trial, at trial, and post-trial) in ensuring that the accused has received a fair trial. The role of the prosecutor is not to obtain a conviction 'at all costs'.

Independence – Prosecutors must act in an independent manner at all times and not be influenced by the wishes of police, a complainant, a victim, a judge or government.

Impartiality – As 'Minister of Justice', prosecutors must apply consistent, objective and transparent considerations in all cases.

The role of prosecutor excludes any notion of winning or losing. The function is a matter of public duty; in civil life there can be none charged with greater personal responsibility. It is to be efficiently performed with an ingrained sense of the dignity, the seriousness and the justness of judicial proceedings.

Above all, the duty of the prosecutor is to ensure a fair trial in accordance with the rule of law:

> Prosecuting counsel in a criminal trial represents the State. The accused, the court and the community are entitled to expect that, in performing the function of presenting the case against an accused, the prosecutor will act with fairness and detachment and always with the objectives of establishing the whole truth in accordance with the procedures and standards which the law requires to be observed, and of helping to ensure that the accused's trial is a fair one.

National guidelines state:

- A prosecutor must fairly assist the court to arrive at the truth, must seek impartially to have the whole of the relevant evidence placed intelligibly before the court, and must seek to assist the court with adequate submissions of law to enable the law to be properly applied to the facts.

- A prosecutor must not press the prosecution's case for a conviction beyond a full and firm presentation of that case.
- A prosecutor must not, by language or other conduct, seek to inflame or bias the court against the accused.
- A prosecutor must not argue any proposition of fact or law which the prosecutor does not believe on reasonable grounds to be capable of contributing to a finding of guilt and also to carry weight.
- A prosecutor must disclose to the opponent as soon as practicable all material available to the prosecutor or of which the prosecutor becomes aware which could constitute evidence relevant to the guilt or innocence of the accused other than material subject to statutory immunity, unless the prosecutor believes on reasonable grounds that such disclosure, or full disclosure, would seriously threaten the integrity of the administration of justice in those proceedings or the safety of any person.
- A prosecutor must call as part of the prosecution's case all witnesses who have relevant and admissible evidence.

Hence prosecutorial duties of impartiality, of full and proper disclosure, of not misleading the court and of calling all relevant witnesses (including those whose evidence may be exculpatory of the guilt of the accused) are particularly important in maintaining the rule of law and the right to a fair trial.

Failure to disclose crucial information undermines the principles of a fair trial.

An example of a case in which the police and prosecutors failed to disclose key information to the defence (another repetitive theme of this book) is discussed in detail in chapter six.

But withholding of key evidence is not just a problem in Australia. In recent years, both prosecutors and police have been accused of systematically concealing information in criminal investigations.

In one example from Tennessee, 18-year-old Noura Jackson was found guilty of murdering her 39-year-old mother Jennifer Jackson, who was stabbed over 50 times in her bedroom at Mendenhall, in East Memphis, in 2005. Evidence against Noura was largely circumstantial, and there was no physical evidence linking her to the murder. One significant element of the prosecution's case was a statement by a key witness, Andrew Hammack, who claimed to have been in a casual sexual relationship with Jackson, and testified that Noura was at the scene of the murder around the time of her mother's death. Hammack also said he had received calls and texts from Noura around the time of her mother's murder. However, in a handwritten note he had given to police, Hammack admitted to having been high on ecstasy on the night in question, and also that he had lent his phone to a friend, so clearly Jackson and he had not been in communication at the time of Jennifer's death. Even though the prosecution has a constitutional obligation to pass on any evidence that may be favourable to the defence, it is in essence a subjective assessment by the prosecution; as no one sees what's in their files – not the defence lawyers, not the judge – it's impossible for the accused to know what evidence may be available to help exonerate them. In Noura's case, the prosecution chose not to reveal the content of the note to the defence, even though it clearly undermined the reliability of Hammack's statement. Noura was found guilty of second-degree murder in February 1991, and sentenced to 20 years and nine months in prison, without the possibility of parole. Noura, like all of the cases of wrongful conviction in this book, had a champion – her defence attorney Valerie Corder, who took the case to the Supreme Court and won. Jackson's murder conviction was overturned, partly on the grounds that the prosecution had failed to disclose the evidence by Hammack that undermined his testimony and previous witness statements. The conviction was therefore deemed unsafe. Noura was still charged with murder, however, so the prosecution offered her a deal known as an Alford plea, to a charge of voluntary manslaughter. An Alford plea is a guilty plea in criminal courts in the US, but is not an admission of guilt. Instead, it allows a defendant to assert their innocence whilst at the same time acknowledge that if the case were to go to trial again, there is likely to be enough information to achieve a conviction. Jackson accepted this deal and, in 2016, after serving 11 years in prison, she was finally released. In August 2019, Jackson spoke about her plea deal, and the fact that she now regrets signing it. She said at the time she took the plea deal she was tired, and saw it as a way of ending her suffering, whilst maintaining her innocence. After a decade-long fight against her murder conviction, this is understandable.

Dr Bob Moles and Associate Professor Bibi Sangha,
lawyers and experts in miscarriages of justice

The importance of the cap being at the flat at the time Pamela was killed cannot be overstated – if this evidence was seen as credible, it meant Andrew was not wearing his orange cap, the headwear he owned, that Katherine Barsden felt was very similar to that worn by the man she'd seen in Flora Metallica from the car. It doesn't rule Mallard out as wearing any headwear that day, as he did own two other bandana-style head dressings, but these were of different colours to the one described and drawn by Katherine.

But was Engelhardt's evidence reliable? Possibly not. Under cross-examination during the trial she admitted that when she first met Andrew she had used a lot of cannabis, and that this had significantly affected her memory at the time of the incident. Her evidence may also have been affected by the fact that she and Mallard were not on the best of terms around the time Pamela was killed, largely because Andrew had been living with Engelhardt for some time, and whilst he had agreed to pay rent he had failed to do so, leading to some bad feeling between the two.

Engelhardt was also troubled by Mallard's behaviour, in that he lied about being an undercover police officer, and even gave her a false name. Both she and the police were so concerned for her safety that during the police's investigation of Pamela's death, and whilst Andrew was still being held at Graylands, the police helped her move out.

Therefore, it can be concluded that, even if it was subconscious, Engelhardt would have been a more favourable Crown witness than a defence witness.

The jury was clearly not convinced by Mallard's version of events, and whilst opportunity to have committed the crime would not be enough to reach a conclusion of guilt, we need to add in the weight of the 'confession evidence'.

At trial in May 1994, a key question the jury had to consider was whether Andrew had confessed at all, and if he had, did they believe this reflected an actual report of what had happened, or was it simply the activity of a disordered mind (Andrew had already spent time in a psychiatric facility; consequently it could be argued this is a significant consideration).

Andrew's explanation for the confessions was that what had appeared to be accounts of events were actually simply hypotheses he was working through in his mind, and – unfortunately for him – expressing out loud to the officers, as he felt he was helping them with their inquiries by offering suggestions as to what might have happened. Other things that appeared in his confession Andrew claimed he had not said at all, rather than being misinterpretations of what he meant, or that if he had said them, it was information fed to him by police rather than statements he voluntarily made to them.

For example, this exchange has been taken from the recorded interview by detectives Brandham and Carter:

Mallard:	If Pamela Lawrence was locking the store up, maybe she came in through the back way; the front door was already locked. Maybe.
Detective:	Okay.
Mallard:	And she left the key in the back door, and that's why he had easy access and that's why she didn't hear him until he was marching down the store.

Mallard also said that, on more than one occasion, his confession was coerced, and that he had been threatened with violence and had also been physically threatened with being killed. He would later claim at appeal that he had only made the drawing after being stripped naked and beaten. So in the end he just told the police what they wanted to hear to end the interviews as quickly as possible.

At trial, he made his disorientation very clear, saying that during the interview on 10 June, he 'was in total confusion to the point where anything he [Caporn] suggested to me I would adopt'.

The trial lasted 10 days, after which time it was clear the jury believed the Crown's version of events, and the explanation that the inconsistencies in the confessions were attempts by Mallard to mislead investigators.

They also believed the prosecution when the Crown lawyer held aloft the picture Andrew had drawn of a wrench and said, 'With this wrench he killed her.' This, with the police and prosecution knowing full well that the forensic pathologist's evidence pre-trial (and never heard by the jury) was that the tool drawn could not have inflicted the injuries Pamela sustained.

Either way, after detectives Brandham and Carter achieved a detailed confession, the jury was convinced of Andrew's guilt beyond reasonable doubt. He was found guilty and sentenced to 20 years in prison.

It was easy for the jury to be sceptical of Mallard and his evidence. He looked so unreliable; his story changing, his memory failing him. But of course, he was unreliable, and we know that people with psychiatric and psychological problems are more vulnerable at every stage of the criminal justice system – they often look guilty when they're not, because of behaviours that fall outside of most people's experience of normal. This makes it even harder for vulnerable people to obtain justice.

FIGHTING FOR JUSTICE

Mallard appealed his conviction, firstly in 1995 when he prepared the documents himself. This appeal was based on the grounds that the original trial judge erroneously admitted into evidence oral conversations between Mallard and police, recorded at the CIB (Criminal Investigation Branch) police office on 10 and 17 June 1994. By the time the appeal was heard, Andrew's legal counsel asked permission to add another five grounds, one of which was that 'new and fresh evidence' had become available since the original trial. This appeal was dismissed in September 1996.

By 2002, Mallard had others interested in his case, notably Colleen Egan, an ex-court reporter and then journalist working as a weekly columnist for the *Sunday Times*, whose help had been enlisted by Andrew's family in 1998 after they desperately reached out to her, hoping she could find fresh evidence that could exonerate him.

Andrew had found his first champion. But there were others to follow.

In turn, Egan was able to enlist the assistance of influential supporters John Quigley MLA (a barrister turned politician, and then shadow Attorney General for WA, as well as the WA Police Union's lawyer for 25 years) and Malcolm McCusker QC (a barrister and Governor of WA from 2011 to 2014), who were both appalled at how the original trial had been conducted.

This was a turning point, as Egan had been working on the case for four years, but hadn't made any significant breakthroughs. When she approached John Quigley, it was a risk. He had, after all, been the counsel of choice for the WA Police Union for many, many years. But Egan knew he was one of the best legal minds available, so took a chance in showing him the information she had.

Quigley was initially reluctant to get involved, but once he did, the tide started to turn for Andrew. Quigley could see problems with the initial prosecution, and also realised that crucial evidence had not been disclosed to the defence.

Quigley also had influence and the power to very publicly draw attention to Andrew's plight. He contacted the then Attorney General and said he was going to make an announcement in Parliament. This was clearly going to prove embarrassing for the Director of Public Prosecutions (DPP), so a deal was struck whereby the

DPP would make available to Quigley everything they had – all of their correspondence and litigation files.

This was unprecedented in Quigley's experience. And the problems were highlighted for him straight away. He was handed a file by staff at the DPP's office with a page that was marked, and was told that 'this should have been shown to the defence, this should have been shown to the court . . . but you should read it now'.

What that page demonstrated was that whilst the lead prosecutor, Ken Bates, was literally telling the court that Mallard murdered Pamela with the wrench he had drawn, a report from the forensic pathologist stated 'that they'd done a test on a pig's head which had convinced the pathologist that a wrench could not have inflicted those injuries'.

Bates had repeated this claim about the wrench 80 times during the 10-day trial, each and every time knowing that this was false and that he was misleading the jury. He also knew the defence had not seen Cooke's report, a breach of the duty of disclosure rules.

In July 2002, Andrew's legal team, led by Quigley, forwarded a petition for clemency to the Attorney General of WA, Jim McGinty, who referred the case to the Court of Criminal Appeal for a new appeal. He was successful, and was granted leave to appeal.

Once this happened, and Andrew had a full legal team working for him, they were able to subpoena documents from WA Police that they could not have got hold of before.

It soon became clear that different versions of statements from witnesses did not match. There were significant inconsistencies that could not be put down to natural variations in memory, yet only the final statement was seen in court, so the disparities were never acknowledged or explained.

This appeal was heard in 2003, and there were a number of grounds: new or fresh evidence was available; non-disclosure by the Crown of important evidence; and the reliability of the confession.

EXPERT INSERT: NEW VERSUS FRESH EVIDENCE

You will often here the terms 'new evidence' or 'fresh evidence' used in relation to criminal appeals.

The first, new evidence, is that which was available at the time of the trial, or would have been discoverable if reasonable attempts had been made.

Fresh evidence refers to that which did not exist at the time of the original trial or was not easily found using due diligence.

The distinction may seem small, but it is important and well established in criminal law. The law indicates that where evidence was available at the time of the original trial (new evidence) then no miscarriage of justice has occurred if there was a failure to call that evidence.

The Court of Criminal Appeal will only consider fresh evidence, and will only quash a conviction where evidence is entered if it shows the appellant to be innocent, or raises such significant doubt about the reliability of the conviction that the guilty verdict should not stand (as in the case of Noura Jackson discussed earlier).

And not all fresh evidence will be considered significant enough to warrant an appeal. To be heard, fresh evidence must be considered by the court to be of such a nature that, when considered in combination with the rest of the information, if it had been heard at the original trial a jury acting reasonably might have acquitted the accused.

A case where new and compelling evidence saw a manslaughter conviction overturned was that of 19-year-old John Button, who was found guilty of killing his girlfriend, 17-year-old Rosemary Anderson in 1963, after it was alleged he ran her over after she got out of the car after the couple had an argument. Button followed her in his car, but she refused to get back in. After a short distance, John stopped to smoke a cigarette, before getting back in the car to find Rosemary. When he caught up with her, he found her lying by the side of the road unconscious and badly injured. She later succumbed to her injuries in hospital.

Button immediately became a suspect, and his stutter made him seem nervous to police. He was interviewed for 22 hours, denied access to legal counsel or his parents, and was hit once by one of the officers interviewing him. After all of that he confessed to hitting Rosemary with his car. He was charged and at trial, evidence of damage to his car was used by the Crown to signify John's guilt. He was convicted of manslaughter and sentenced to five years in prison.

For decades Button protested his innocence, but the key evidence against him – damage to the front of his car – supposedly spoke to his guilt.

That is until 2002, when Western Australia's Court of Criminal Appeal quashed Button's conviction on the basis that serial killer Eric Edgar Cooke had murdered Rosemary – who confessed to the crime many times.

Cooke's admissions had always been ignored, until Cooke (who had been on a murder spree at the time of Rosemary's death, which comprised 22 violent crimes, eight resulting in deaths) again confessed on the Bible 10 minutes before his execution by hanging to Rosemary's and another murder, that of 22-year-old Jillian Brewer. Cooke was the last person to be hanged in Western Australia, with the sentence being carried out on 26 October 1964.

Other evidence that was new was entered during his appeals hearing that supported Button's innocence. Firstly, Trevor Condron, the police officer who originally examined John's car after Rosemary's death, told the court that whilst the car was damaged, it was not consistent with hitting a person. Also new to the appeal was the fact that three weeks before Rosemary's death, Button had reported another accident that could easily account for the damage found. The police knew about this report, but had not thought it relevant to the case, and had dismissed it. The defence was not made aware of it during the original trial. The court also heard new medical evidence from a doctor who had treated Anderson, who stated that her injuries were not consistent with Button's car. Another expert in pedestrian accidents was asked to review the physical injuries Rosemary sustained and compare the trauma to the damage on both Button's car and the vehicle Cooke claimed to have been driving at the time. It was found the injuries could have been sustained by Cooke's car but not John's vehicle, supporting Cooke's confession to killing Rosemary.

Without the new and compelling evidence John Button would likely have remained in prison for killing Rosemary. Instead, he now heads up Western Australia's innocence initiative (see page 201 for more on innocence initiatives).

By the time the appeal was heard, Engelhardt had become an even more difficult witness, although the reasons for this were not made clear to the defence until the second appeal – Engelhardt claimed that during the investigation into Pamela's murder, police told her that if she was 'helpful' with their inquiries they would drop a charge against her relating to being in possession of drug paraphernalia. This didn't happen, and she later swore an affidavit to this effect, at which time she was evidently annoyed at the police for not dropping the charge.

Her evidence at appeal was not very helpful to anyone, as by this time many people had tried to talk to her about the case from both sides – this included Andrew's defence lawyers, a writer, a journalist, and a prison chaplain, all of whom appeared to believe Mallard was not guilty, as well as detectives concerned about the allegations in the affidavit regarding police coercion. So, when questioned at appeal, she was unhelpful and confused, contradicting herself, and frustrated with the whole process. She just wanted it to be over, stating that 'I really can't remember anything'.

The appellate judges reviewed the evidence, including Engelhardt's testimony regarding the hat, which at various times she said may or may not have been over the door the day Pamela was killed, and determined there was no new evidence, dismissing the first ground of appeal.

They also looked at the effects of non-disclosure by the Crown, both of the drawings done by Katherine Barsden, and information relating to the clothes Andrew was wearing that day. This was important, as the report prepared by the principal chemist at the forensic laboratory, a Mr Lynch who tested the clothing, revealed that the salts detected were inconsistent with the river water provided for comparison, taken from the same spot as indicated by Mallard where he said he had rinsed them. Lynch even tested new clothes, soaked in the same river water in question, then re-enacted heavy rainfall to see if it could wash away the all traces of the river water. His conclusion was that rain would not have removed all traces of the river water.

So it looks like this is also untrue: Mallard had not washed the blood out of his clothes in the river.

This report should obviously have been provided to the defence, as it contradicted Mallard's confession, making it even less reliable, but it wasn't. Yet another failure of disclosure by the prosecution.

Sometimes it's the evidence that's missing that's key. So the appeal then turned its attention to the DNA evidence, in the form of the blood you would expect to have been found on Andrew's clothes as a result of the significant blood spatter at the scene – as supported by Dr Cooke's evidence, the forensic pathologist who performed Pamela's post-mortem, and who said there would be 'heavy spatter' on the arms and hands of the offender. There was also likely to have been blood spatter on the lower half of the assailant's trousers at the front, due to a number of blows having been delivered whilst Pamela was on the ground.

New tests were done, searching for traces of DNA, which were more sensitive than those available in 1994 that had failed to find any trace of Pamela's blood on Mallard's clothes. Again, the tests found nothing, and although this was considered by the appellate judges as 'fresh' evidence, as it in essence gave the same result as those presented at the original trial, this was not considered relevant. And as Mallard had stated that he already washed at least two of the four items tested in fresh water prior to the police taking them for forensic evaluation, both the issues raised over the river water and lack of blood spatter were dismissed.

Another key point the judges considered was relevant to the appeal was Mallard's mental health at the time the confession was taken, as the defence now had evidence of psychiatric illness, provided in affidavits by a Dr Stephen Patchett. But this wasn't considered 'fresh evidence', given that a forensic psychiatrist, Dr Jeremy O'Dea, had already provided a report, prepared for the original trial, that Mallard was suffering from bipolar disorder (a condition made worse by cannabis use), so the issues over Andrew's psychological stability were clearly established. O'Dea was well placed to assess Andrew, as he had treated him at Graylands Hospital both before and after he was interviewed about Pamela's murder.

The only variation between the evidence of the two psychiatrists was that Dr Patchett described Mallard's condition as 'unipolar' as opposed to 'bipolar'. The key difference being that those suffering from bipolar disorder have highs and lows, with the highs being described as mania, which can lead to feelings of euphoria or impulsive behaviours, amongst other effects. Those with unipolar disorder do not experience the manic highs.

What is important is that the jury never heard Dr O'Dea's evidence that Mallard was suffering from a psychiatric condition, and the psychiatrist would later tell the Corruption and Crime Commission – when this all blew up in 2007 – that his patient was having problems separating fact from fiction at the time he confessed to Pamela's murder. He went on to add that Mallard's bipolar condition should have raised significant doubts over the reliability of his admissions, which O'Dea would have spoken to had he been called as a witness during the trial. But he wasn't; only his written report was entered as evidence.

The appeal judges acknowledged that it might have been useful to hear the psychiatric evidence during the trial, but did not consider it a ground for overturning the conviction.

They also accepted the uncontested fact that the DPP had intentionally withheld evidence from the defence. However, all grounds for appeal were considered and discounted, and the appeal dismissed, as they found the new evidence did not change the case against him.

This was a huge blow.

The outcome: a man was still in prison for a murder he did not commit.

Mallard's family was in limbo, unable to comprehend how the criminal justice system, which is meant to protect citizens, could be failing so badly.

And Quigley, who had gone out on a limb challenging the police Union by accusing WA police members of misconduct, was being vilified. The police Union turned on him, and even members of his own family thought he was crazy for taking on such a controversial case against his previous employers.

He also had his reputation as a politician to consider.

Egan was also having her professional judgment questioned, as people thought she'd put her career on the line supporting a murderer.

But none of the personal or professional fallout was going to stop Andrew's supporters from continuing to fight for him, and for justice.

In October 2004 Mallard's legal team, still working pro bono, including Quigley and McCusker, was granted special leave via the Attorney General to appeal to the High Court – this was Mallard's last avenue of legal redress. They were successful, and on 6–7 September 2005, Andrew's second appeal was heard.

A great deal was made of the fact that officers investigating Pamela's murder withheld evidence from the defence that they were in possession of before the trial, and that this was in breach of the *Director of Public Prosecutions Act 1991* (WA), which specifically states that:

Disclosure of Information to the Defence

59. When information which may be exculpatory comes to the attention of a prosecutor and the prosecutor does not intend adducing that evidence, the prosecutor will disclose the evidence . . . These details should be disclosed in good time.

The appeal judges went on to add that the prosecution must also disclose all relevant evidence to the accused, and failure to do so may result in a verdict being quashed.

The court now turned its attention to inconsistencies in statements that could have weakened the confession evidence. Such as the contradictions between Andrew's and the taxi driver Peverall's accounts of timings. Peverall's evidence was that Andrew had told him he was going inside to get the money to pay the fare, but that he did not return. The taxi driver waited for about 20 minutes before returning to his taxi rank, taking another call at 5:22pm. Andrew had confirmed part of this, saying that he had lied to get out of paying the fare as he intended to abscond, and on entering the flats had crossed through to another building where he went to an upper floor to look out of a window to see if the taxi was still there. He said he waited around 20 minutes, then walked from the Bel Air flats to Pamela's jewellery shop. Whichever route Andrew took, he would've needed to walk straight past where the taxi was waiting, and as the driver was clearly looking out for him but did not see him, this could not have happened.

This is crucial – it's Andrew's alibi, even if he didn't realise it, confirmed by an independent eyewitness, Peverall. If Andrew was at the flats at 5pm–5:20pm he was not at the jewellery shop bludgeoning Pamela to death.

The judges were also deeply unimpressed with the fact that only 20 minutes of 11 hours of interviews were recorded, describing this as 'inexplicable'.

The problems with the Crown case were noted, and the appellate judges concluded by saying that 'The Court of Criminal Appeal, in deciding the issues raised in the appellant's petition, erred both in its approach and in its conclusions. The appellant's conviction must be quashed', and a retrial was ordered. This decision was based on the fact that the police and prosecutors had clearly withheld evidence from the court and the defence. Specifically, this related to Detective Sergeant Mal Shervill and Detective Constable David Caporn, as well as Crown prosecutor Ken Bates.

Even with all the concerns raised, the DPP waited another six months to drop the charges against Andrew, and on 20 February 2006 – after serving more than 12 years in prison for a murder he did not commit – Mallard was released.

But the Crown was still not completely letting go. In a statement released announcing the discontinuation of the prosecution, as some evidence was no longer admissible, the DPP, Robert Cock QC, made clear that Andrew remained the primary suspect in Pamela's death, and that if any new evidence came to light in the future that would reasonably lead to a successful conviction, they would re-try him.

They still could not admit they were wrong.

This fuelled further problems for Andrew, as the public felt a murderer had been released. Pamela Lawrence's family were fearful they would run in to him in Perth, as they still believed him to be a violent killer. This really scared them.

In 2010 Mallard would speak for the first time about his ordeal to Colleen Egan, for a documentary called *The Wronged Man*.

During the interview with Egan, Andrew describes how vulnerable he was, and how he became an easy target for unscrupulous police to pin Pamela's murder on: 'I was down on my luck. I was vulnerable. I was living on the streets. I was trying to survive'.

He spoke of the years of psychotherapy to help him deal with his ordeal, the onset of post-traumatic stress disorder, panic attacks and the ongoing impact on his life and health.

THE ALTERNATIVE SUSPECT

After the DPP announced it was not pursuing the case against Mallard, the Commissioner of Police decided to see if a cold case review of Pamela's murder was warranted.

The WA Police Commissioner, Karl O'Callaghan, wanted new eyes across the evidence. New techniques brought to bear where possible. He had no preconceptions. He was searching for the truth.

As part of that search, a British cold case expert and forensic scientist, David Barclay (famed for his involvement with the review of the inquiry into the Claremont serial murders, which oversaw the deaths of three young women from Claremont, WA, in 1996 and 1997, as well as the sexual assault of two others in 1995), was enlisted to assist with the reinvestigation.

The team tasked with re-examining the case quickly noted a key piece of evidence either overlooked or ignored by the original investigators – a palm print taken from a glass-topped display case in the shop. This was highly significant for two reasons: 1) the staff were in the habit of wiping this particular surface down after every customer left, so this likely belonged to the last person in the shop before Pamela was killed, and 2) even more importantly, when the print was run against those in the fingerprint database (which also includes palm prints) it came back as a match to someone else – violent criminal Simon Rochford. Rochford also more closely matched the description Katherine gave of the man she saw in the shop.

It is simply mind-blowing that the police did not follow this lead earlier, as Rochford was in prison for the brutal murder of his girlfriend, Brigitta Dickens, on 15 July 1994. Dickens had been beaten to death by a weapon specifically fashioned by Rochford for the purpose – he attached a steel collar, such as those used to attach body building weights to a bar, to a broom handle.

Despite an extensive search of police exhibits and evidence, the actual collar itself used in Brigitta's murder could not be located in 2006 when the cold case team was conducting its reinvestigation of Pamela's death. However, photographs and dimensions were available, and the weapon was consistent with the injures found on her head.

There was more forensic evidence directly linking Rochford to Pamela's murder. The photographs of the collar showed that it had been painted blue, relevant as blue flecks of paint were recovered from Pamela's head wounds but no source had been discovered at her shop, thus indicating they had been transferred from the weapon. A rucksack belonging to Rochford was subsequently found, and inside were flecks of paint that were chemically identical to those recovered from Pamela's head. (The weapon was found in 2013 after an audit of exhibits, and the blue paint of the weapon matched those from Rochford's backpack and recovered from Pamela's head. This provided further corroboration that Rochford was guilty of murdering Pamela.)

Rochford was never held to account for Pamela's death, because on 19 May, hours after he was named as a person of interest in the case, he was found dead in his cell at Albany Regional Prison, Western Australia, having committed suicide.

More incredible still, the cold case review came across another important witness, who again was in the files all along. Artist Lloyd Peirce was living in a flat near Flora Metallica. The night Pamela was killed he saw a man fleeing the scene. He was running fast across Stirling Highway and was almost hit by a passing taxi. He drew up short and put his hands on the bonnet to steady himself. In that moment the man's behaviour struck Peirce as so odd that he made a sketch of the man on the back of the painting he was working on.

When he heard about the attack on Pamela he went to the police.

Caporn came to speak to Peirce, but not simply to interview him. He immediately made it obvious they considered him a suspect in the attack. As soon as Lloyd realised this, he stopped talking.

That was the end of a promising lead, until the cold case review, during which Peirce was re-interviewed, and amazingly he still had the drawing which he now handed over to police. It bore a striking resemblance to Rochford.

If the police had tracked down Rochford after Pamela's murder, they may have been able to prevent him from going on to kill his girlfriend Brigitta seven weeks later. In that sense, the fixation on Andrew Mallard as the culprit in Pamela's murder is also potentially responsible for another young woman's death.

THE CORRUPTION AND CRIME COMMISSION 2008

Following the cold case review into Pamela's murder, and the clear evidence that another man was the likely offender, John Quigley referred the case to the Corruption and Crime Commission (CCC), which announced it would be investigating. Public hearings subsequently began on 31 July 2007 and in the meantime the CCC requested that the full cold case report not be released, either publicly or internally, and specifically that police involved in the original investigation were not allowed to see it.

The CCC's remit was to determine if any member of the WA police or prosecutors behaved either unethically or illegally in regards to the Mallard investigation and prosecution.

This was yet another risk John Quigley was taking with this career. In 2007 he used parliamentary privilege to name two undercover police officers. He did this in defence of claims of misconduct against him made to the CCC, whereby he stood accused of using his position to threaten a former undercover police agent with exposure if he didn't help to clear Andrew Mallard when Quigley first became involved in Andrew's case in 2002.

Quigley countered by saying he was simply getting one of the undercover officers, only identified as 'Gary' at the CCC inquiry, to come forward and tell the truth about the covert aspect of the investigation.

On 29 November Quigley revealed the two officers' identities, one of whom was a protected witness for the CCC, and publicly rejected the suggestions he had acted inappropriately. In his powerful statement to Parliament, Quigley said, 'Ultimately, when the courts fail, the police department and the courts all failed . . . this is the last stop in democracy. You come here.'

As a further result, in 2007 his life membership of the WA Police Union was cancelled, as he was now seen as the enemy.

After 83 days of both private and public hearings and five million public dollars later, on 7 October 2008 the Commission was ready to hand down its findings. And they were damning. Up to around 12 police officers were facing possible adverse findings, but in the end only three were identified by the CCC as having engaged in misconduct with regards to Andrew's prosecution.

The Commission recommended that disciplinary action be taken against two assistant chief police commissioners, Mal Shervill and David Caporn (both of whom had been promoted to this senior rank in the intervening years since Mallard's prosecution), as well as the deputy director of public prosecution, Ken Bates, who was the prosecutor at Mallard's trial. In total, the Commission made four misconduct findings against Shervill, and two against both Caporn and Bates.

Pamela Lawrence's family was left reeling. Katie Kingdon, Pamela's daughter, would later give an interview expressing her shock at the outcome, particularly as Mal Shervill had been so personable and warm to her family throughout their ordeal. This caused the family additional trauma as they struggled to accept this new reality that things were not at all as they had seemed with the prosecution.

The Director of Public Prosecutions, Robert Cock QC, asked Ken Bates to step down from his position at the DPP.

The police acted quickly, and the same day the findings were released the WA Police Commissioner, Karl O'Callaghan, immediately served Shervill and Caporn with a loss of confidence notice; this is a significant act, and one a Commissioner of Police will only take when they do not have confidence in a member's suitability to continue in their role, taking into consideration their integrity, honesty, conduct, performance, or competence. Both were subsequently stood down, but on full pay whilst the Commissioner awaited the two men's formal, written response to the CCC's report.

O'Callaghan was prevented from taking matters further, however, as he received legal advice from the State Solicitor's office that he was not allowed to question Shervill and Caporn as a result of the CCC's report, but rather he had to conduct his own internal inquiry. This, regardless of the fact the CCC had been overseen by a learned judge over a period of 15 months.

In the end, Shervill and Caporn never faced the full consequences of their parts in the wrongful conviction of Andrew Mallard, as they both resigned, preventing any police disciplinary action going forward; Shervill resigning the day before he was due to answer the Police Commissioner's questions.

Caporn had left earlier, to take a $130,000 a year job with the Fire and Emergency Services Authority, his clean work record intact.

This left Karl O'Callaghan deeply frustrated, and in an interview for *The West Australian* on 4 October 2010, he described the CCC's inquiry as 'completely pointless' as he could not take any effective action against the officers found guilty of misconduct, and that he considered the matter unresolved.

An innocent man had spent over 12 years in prison, and yet the officers who set in motion a miscarriage of justice would never be fully held to account. This, sadly, is a pattern we will see again and again as we move through the cases in this book.

O'Callaghan felt this outcome was unsatisfactory for Mallard and his family, Pamela and her family, as well as the community, as it could hardly be seen to help restore faith and confidence in due process. There was also no resolution for WA Police.

It didn't need to end this way. If the CCC had found that any officer had acted corruptly or committed an illegal act, the process of redress would have been much cleaner. However, as they were only found guilty of misconduct, the onus then falls back on the employer to investigate and take any disciplinary action thereafter. If the individuals in question then leave that employ, there really is little that can be done.

In May 2009, Andrew received $3.25 million in compensation from the State Government. He still had the option of pursuing Bates, Shervill and Caporn in a civil action.

And more injustice was still to come.

In 2010, the State Administrative Tribunal in Western Australia, the state's legal watchdog, announced it was taking action against Quigley for releasing the names and contact details of the undercover police officers involved in the covert operation investigation of Andrew Mallard for Pamela's murder.

John Quigley stood accused of bringing the legal profession into disrepute. There were three complaints against him in total, and on 2 November 2011 he was found guilty and fined $3000 for professional misconduct, but the Tribunal did not revoke his licence to practise law. This was bad, but it could have been worse. The maximum fine he could have received was $25,000, and he also faced a term of suspension from legal practice, or in the absolute worst case scenario, a recommendation that the Supreme Court should disbar him.

It is astonishing to note that the only person facing professional charges as a result of this debacle is a man – a champion of justice – who helped clear an innocent man of murder.

IN THE END . . .

It was a long road to justice for Mallard. Had it not been for the Corruption and Crime Commission's reinvestigation, pushed for by Andrew's supporters, Mallard would in the eyes of the DPP and the public have remained a murderer at large.

This fight for justice for Andrew Mallard placed a massive strain on him and his family.

But also mixed up in this was Pamela Lawrence's family, who for many years felt as though no one cared about them and their loss. From the outside, it appeared as if a group of influential people was trying to free Pamela's murderer from prison. Her family believed in the reliability of the justice system, as high profile people from the WA police and the prosecutor's office were still telling them they had the right man behind bars.

It wasn't until years later, when Simon Rochford was identified as Pamela's likely murderer, and members of the original investigative team were found to have been guilty of misconduct, that the family realised just how badly the system had let them all down.

The pain for them goes on, and was greatly exacerbated by the legal battles that lasted years, a constant reminder of the brutal way Pamela died.

And all totally unnecessary.

If the police had simply analysed the evidence in front of them, the palm print and eyewitness testimony could have led them to the offender. Instead, they focused on a vulnerable man, coercing a false confession and withholding evidence. Together with the actions of the DPP, policing at its worst led to Andrew losing 12 years of his life and another young woman dying at the hands of Pamela's killer.

But there's a little light in all of this dark.

In 2019, the *Criminal Appeals Amendment Bill 2019* was passed, giving those found guilty of a crime a second chance of redress through the State's highest court, where new and compelling evidence has been discovered since the original trial. This change largely transpired because of John Quigley's involvement with Andrew's fight for justice, after Mallard's case was initially rejected by the Court of Appeal. In Andrew's case, a second appeal was only possible following an application being made directly to the Attorney General.

Sadly, when the final touches were being put to the Bill in April 2019, Andrew was killed by a teenage hit-and-run driver in Los Angeles, so he never saw the legal changes that may help others in the future come to fruition. But this is, nonetheless, a positive legacy for a man who suffered so much at the hands of the Australian criminal justice system.

FOUR

HENRY KEOGH:
THE MURDER THAT NEVER HAPPENED
(1994)

'How long can you be a daughter without a father? . . .
How long can hope survive without justice?'

Alexis Keogh, Henry's daughter, speaking to
The Sydney Morning Herald in 2014

As we have seen, miscarriages of justice can happen for many reasons – evidence can be planted by unscrupulous police or missed due to incompetence, or experts employed to assist the courts to interpret evidence might get it wrong.

The latter of these came into play in South Australia across a spate of miscarriages of justice, all linked to the work of one forensic pathologist, Dr Colin Manock. Manock's evidence was manifestly wrong and misleading in a whole range of cases, and potentially led to persons guilty of crimes not being prosecuted as well as innocent people being accused and found guilty of crimes they did not commit.

The public was first informed about a number of potential wrongful conviction cases in South Australia in the ABC's *Four Corners* episode, 'Expert Witness', in October 2001. To date there have been over 130 radio and television programs on these issues. This chapter will review three of Manock's heart-rending errors, highlighted in an inquiry into the deaths of three babies – Storm Deane, Billy Barnard, and Joshua Nottle – to illustrate the damage one expert can do to the lives of so many, before focusing on the case of Henry Keogh, who was found guilty of murdering his fiancée, Anna-Jane Cheney, by drowning.

Keogh spent 20 years in prison for a murder that never happened; Anna-Jane's death was a tragic accident.

THE BABY DEATHS

In 1994–1995 the Coroner in Adelaide conducted an inquiry into three baby deaths; one baby was three months of age and the other two were nine months. Each child had died in separate, unrelated incidents. The link between them was that Dr Manock had undertaken the post-mortem (PM) in each case, and said all three had died of bronchopneumonia, a basic lung infection and very easy for a pathologist to diagnose.

In each death, the finding of bronchopneumonia was unsupported and each of the babies had 'quite extensive injuries'. Yet still Manock had concluded that the children died of natural causes. The police and doctors at the hospitals where the children were admitted prior to death did not agree, and were concerned that serious child abuse, potentially even murder, was taking place and going undiagnosed.

The concerns of police and medical professionals were made known to the Coroner, Mr Wayne Chivell, who decided the best course of action was to hold an inquest, looking at all three deaths simultaneously.

Storm Dean lived with his parents, Heather and Craig, who stated that on Thursday 16 October 1992, Craig told the Coroner that he had picked three-month old Storm up by the scruff of his clothing and 'flipped him' about two feet onto the bed. Craig said that he treated all of his children this way, as this would somehow help them in later life. He also admitted to having squeezed baby Storm around the chest to 'teach him how to breathe from the chest'. After the flip onto the bed, Craig and Heather gave evidence that they went outside, returning later to find Storm pale and unresponsive. They tried to resuscitate him, but were unsuccessful and called an ambulance. When the crew arrived, Storm had no heartbeat and wasn't breathing. He was taken to hospital and placed on life support, but the following morning the decision was made to turn off his ventilator.

The Coroner was told that Craig's behaviour had been unusual at the hospital, in that when the life support was turned off he put his thumb in the baby's mouth, saying that he did not like to see him gasping for breath. The doctor present was disturbed by this, but concluded it did not contribute to Storm's death. But two of the doctors, taking Craig's odd behaviour into account, were concerned enough that they contacted the consultant paediatric pathologist at the hospital, who arranged for a full post-mortem to be undertaken. Dr Manock undertook the post-mortem, and gave bronchopneumonia as the cause of death. Manock completely failed, however, to note two potential skull fractures and four broken ribs.

Dr Anthony Thomas, an independent forensic pathologist appointed by the Coroner as part of the inquiry, reviewed the material, and from the evidence available in Storm's death he determined that Manock had failed to do basic aspects of a post-mortem – including weighing or microscopic examination of organs, nor did he weigh or measure Storm's body or undertake an analysis of the eyes (a classic sign of a baby being shaken is evidence of ruptured blood vessels in the eyes, which can be seen if dissected during the PM). He concluded that bronchopneumonia was not the cause of death, and that the injuries were not natural. An expert in neuropathology later examined Storm's brain and determined there may have been damage to the brain stem (which can be caused by a 'whiplash' type injury resultant from severe shaking as the infant's neck hyperflexes and hyperextends).

The Coroner appeared shocked that, given Manock's experience, he had totally failed to undertake the appropriate tests to exclude non-accidental injury as the cause of Storm's death.

Damningly, at the conclusion of his investigation into Storm's death, the Coroner said that 'The post-mortem examination achieved the *opposite* of what should have been its purpose – it *closed off* lines of investigation rather than opening them up'.

Storm's cause of death was then recorded as undetermined, but the Coroner also said that there was still time to review his death appropriately, and to put things right.

Dr Thomas then turned his attention to Billy Barnard's death as part of the Coronial inquiry. Billy's parents, Cherry and David, had given evidence that nine-month-old Billy was found not breathing on the morning of 31 July 1993, after spending the night in a sleeping bag with his mum. Cherry called an ambulance and Billy was rushed to hospital, but was pronounced deceased shortly after arrival. This was not the first of Cherry and David's children to die. Billy's elder sister had died at three weeks old, again whilst sleeping with her mother in a sleeping bag – a fact one of the ambulance officers remembered, as he had also attended the first call out to Billy's sister. The ambulance crew gave evidence that Cherry seemed 'detached', though of course this could be a result of shock as people respond very differently in such stressful situations, which was the same reaction she had exhibited on the first occasion. However, the ambulance officer gave evidence that in his experience it was such an unusual reaction that he mentioned his concerns to the medical authorities when they reached the hospital.

The Coroner heard that the family was well known to Child Protection Services, and Cherry admitted to having 'cracked and snapped' Billy's arm. There was significant evidence of neglect and poor parenting skills, and David, Billy's father, had been found guilty for assaulting a child in an earlier relationship.

The Department of Family and Community Services (renamed Children, Youth and Family Services in 1998) clearly let Billy down, as he was obviously in danger.

But they weren't the only ones.

Dr Manock did the autopsy, and again the Coroner found that he failed to undertake basic analyses such as weighing Billy's organs, including the lungs, which Dr Thomas later said would have provided crucial evidence, given that Manock gave bronchopneumonia as a cause of death – without a full examination of the key organ affected – a finding which, under the circumstances, is in my view inexplicable.

The Coroner agreed, and as with Storm's death, he concluded that the autopsy undertaken by Manock did not achieve its purpose, i.e. to provide information to investigators to help them decide what course to follow, and that the investigation was ended before it had begun as the diagnosis offered gave the investigation no focus. Billy had been subjected to 'severe and extended neglect'. Most seriously, he had a broken arm, which had been left untreated for between two and four weeks. He had severe nappy rash, to the extent that his penis was encrusted and inflamed. Clearly Billy was being maltreated.

Given that this was the second death in similar circumstances in the same family with a history of violence and neglect, the lack of a proper investigation was disturbing.

The final child death case to be reviewed for the Coronial inquiry was that of nine-month-old Joshua Nottle, who on 17 August 1993 was found dead in his cot by his parents, Julie-Ann and Sean. He was taken to hospital, but was dead on arrival with horrific injuries from child abuse. At hospital, various signs of trauma were noted. He was literally covered in bruises, and 15 rib fractures were clearly visible on X-ray and showed signs of healing – indicating he had suffered multiple episodes of physical abuse. There was also a severe fracture of the spinal column. As a result of doctors' concerns, detectives from the Criminal Investigation Branch (CIB) attended.

The police interviewed the parents, after which Sean was charged with the baby's murder, and Joshua's body was submitted for post-mortem examination by Dr Manock.

The CIB officers were in attendance at the Forensic Science Centre, which is in Adelaide, during the autopsy, as they were clearly highly suspicious that the death was not natural. Following PM, and all of the clear evidence of physical abuse, Manock gave the cause of death as bronchopneumonia.

The CIB officers were concerned about the finding and spoke to Manock, who explained that simply throwing a child in the air and catching them could cause rib fractures, and he disregarded the spinal fractures as evidence of resuscitation attempts by Sean. The police were still dissatisfied with this explanation, and spoke to the Director of Child Protection Services at the hospital, Dr Terry Donald, who disagreed that these innocent acts described by Manock could have caused the trauma found at PM. He stated that the degree of force necessary to cause those injuries was far greater than Manock suggested, and the spinal injury Joshua sustained was more typical of victims of high-speed car accidents, particularly if a child has been expelled from a moving vehicle.

A specialist in child pathology, Dr Roger Byard, also examined Joshua's results, and was of the opinion that the rib fractures were likely the result of being squeezed by an adult, and that the spinal fracture was not the result of resuscitation attempts and was unlikely to have been accidental. He also said that the lung weights given by Manock did not support the diagnosis of bronchopneumonia.

Dr Manock did dissect Joshua's eyes, looking for signs of ruptured blood vessels that would have been evidence of shaking, but only at the insistence of Dr Donald. No haemorrhages were detected.

Again, Dr Thomas found the basic body and organ weights had not been recorded, except Joshua's lungs. No microscopic examination was performed on the areas of bruising, or the deceased's brain. Manock did note the rib fractures, but missed fractures of both clavicles (collar bones), which were clearly visible on X-ray. Dr Thomas stated that bronchopneumonia was an unlikely cause of death, and that in his view the PM was inadequate.

However, at the time of Joshua's death, because of Manock's findings, the police downgraded the charges against Sean from murder to serious assault. Later they would say that had they had the information provided by Dr Thomas earlier, the charge of murder would have stood, and the case would have been investigated very differently. It is a prime example of how the weight attributed to this evidence had a heavy impact on the decision-making process in the case.

EXPERT INSERT: THE WEIGHT OF EVIDENCE

The weight that should be attributed to any piece of evidence in a criminal investigation is comprised of two elements – the forensic examiner's assessment as to the likelihood that a piece of evidence at a crime scene originated from a particular source (i.e. the probability that DNA taken from a murder scene matches DNA from a suspect), combined with how important that evidence is in suggesting the guilt or otherwise of the defendant.

The first step, the examiner's evaluation, is extremely important, as they choose what evidence to collect and what to process; the weight they attribute to the evidence will be highly influential on a jury.

The forensic science community, in response to concerns raised by the wider scientific fraternity as well as the general public, has increasingly been looking for ways to quantify methods for applying appropriate weight to evidence, and many do this by providing a 'likelihood ratio', which aims to be an objective way of conveying the meaning to others.

Using DNA as an example, as one of the core forensic sciences, generally speaking when a DNA 'match' is achieved and a likelihood ratio attached to allow for the weight that should be placed on it, if the likelihood ratio is high the jury can be reasonably assured that the suspect and the offender are the same person.

An example of how powerful DNA matches can be is the Tasmanian case of Bradley Scott Purkiss, who murdered Dwayne Davies in 2017, wrapping his body in a blue tarp before disposing of it in a shallow grave. Purkiss and Dwayne's wife, Margaret Otto, were jointly found guilty of his murder. DNA expert Rita Westbury told the court that Purkiss' DNA was found on twine that had been tied around Dwayne's body, and that, 'It is 100 billion times more likely Bradley Purkiss is a contributor to that profile than he is not.' This is the highest possible in terms of DNA matches, and is clearly a very powerful statistic in the minds of the jurors, and when reliable (and I am not suggesting it is not in this case), a useful indicator of what weight should be afforded to that evidence in relation to the rest of the case.

But DNA matches can also lead to erroneous convictions, and ultimately miscarriages of justice. And once your DNA is 'matched' to a scene it can be almost impossible to demonstrate successfully that either there has been an error, as most lay people (including those that sit on juries) believe a DNA match equals guilt beyond reasonable doubt.

A case that exemplifies the misappropriation of very high likelihood ratios in criminal cases by an expert witness is that of Sir Roy Meadow, who gave evidence in a number of child death cases in the UK in the late 1990s and early 2000s, where women were accused of murdering their own children. Meadow became famous for his maxim that 'One [child death in a family] is a tragedy, two is suspicious, and three is murder unless there is proof to the contrary'. In addition to this, Meadow provided erroneous statistical evidence in court – that the likelihood of two children dying of Sudden Infant Death Syndrome in the same family is 73,000,000:1. He reached this extraordinary figure by simply squaring the chances of one child dying (8500:1). I won't go into the mathematical intricacies of why this is unsound, but needless to say there is no scientific or statistical basis for this figure, as many experts strongly asserted. Nevertheless, this 'fact' was heard by the jury in a number of cases where women had been accused of murdering a number of their own children, and was a significant factor in them being found guilty as very high weight would have been attributed to Meadow's evidence by the jury – how could it not be murder with odds like that? These cases were later overturned, but the damage caused by Meadow and his flawed statistics had been done.

All of these child deaths were tragic. The Coroner concluded the inquest by saying that, of the three, Joshua's injuries were the most obviously non-accidental. The Coroner also said that Joshua's father should have been facing murder charges, but because of Manock, there was no causative link between the injury and the child's death. This had a direct impact on the investigation. Sadly, because the requisite tests and examinations were not undertaken at autopsy, the Coroner and police may have had grave suspicions about how Joshua came by his injuries, but nothing could be proven.

The Coroner described some of Manock's responses to questions asked at the inquiry as 'spurious'.

Counsel assisting the Coroner said that 'the weight of medical opinion is the finding of bronchial pneumonia in each case was not an appropriate finding'. He said there were other possible causes of death, and in each case 'at least one possibility was homicide'. He said 'the findings were not satisfactorily supported by the evidence and this was cause for concern'.

Counsel said it was 'beyond doubt' that someone in the house where Joshua lived had caused him 'terrible injuries and may well have actively killed him'.

Joshua's mother has repeatedly pleaded for an inquiry into the death of her son. Despite the open acknowledgment that he may well have been murdered, the names of these babies do not appear on the lists of unsolved crimes, and there has been no attempt to make those responsible for these deaths accountable.

The Attorney General of South Australia, Vickie Chapman MHA, has openly acknowledged Dr Manock's role in these appalling cases. In an ABC Adelaide radio interview in July 2018, she said:

… there are a number of baby cases, for example, where reports were given by Mr [sic] Manock. I can recall one where there was a decision of a child, an infant, ostensibly dying of pneumonia but then had massive bruising over the child's body.

However, she has told Joshua's mother that she is not in a position to initiate any inquiry into his death or into the conduct of Dr Manock in relation to these matters.

THE CORONER'S ERROR

The baby deaths inquiry was finalised shortly before another important trial in Colin Manock's career – that of Henry Keogh, in 1995 for murder. Surely, as Manock was so widely discredited, this would have impacted on the reliability of his evidence in Henry's case – as Manock was the Crown's star expert witness.

Unfortunately, the Coroner decided to 'delay publishing the Findings' in the baby deaths until the Keogh trial had been resolved. He chose to do this because he was 'sensitive' to the fact that Keogh's trial was proceeding at the time, and that Manock was a principal Crown witness against him. So, to avoid a mistrial, he decided to delay publishing the Findings until after Keogh's trial had concluded.

To my mind this in itself represents a miscarriage of justice, as had the jury in Keogh's case been aware of the significant questions over Manock's credibility, the outcome may have been very different.

However, the Crown has a duty to disclose any material or information that may reflect on the credibility of a witness in a criminal trial. The Coroner had not only found that Dr Manock had made errors in the baby death cases, but also that in answer to some of his questions on oath, Dr Manock had given responses which were disingenuous.

There had of course been previous indications of such concerns reported in the media, which may be said to have put Mr Keogh's defence 'on notice'. But a formal finding in a report by a Coroner, a judicial officer, would be far more important, and impactful.

As it was, the court did not hear about the problems in the baby deaths inquiry, and Keogh was convicted of murder.

Just two days later, on 25 August 1995, the 93-page Coronial Findings were released. From that moment, Keogh had an impeccable argument for his conviction to be overturned. Yet, it took him over 20 years to achieve that result. An astonishing failure of the legal system. It also raises the question about potential miscarriages of justice in other cases Manock has been involved with.

Let's look at the Keogh case more closely to see exactly what went wrong and what lessons can be learnt.

HENRY KEOGH AND COLIN MANOCK

The happy couple, Anna-Jane Cheney and Henry Keogh, must have looked to all the world as if they had a wonderful future waiting for them, engaged and only weeks away from their wedding, scheduled for 24 April 1994.

Everything was going well in their world. Wedding plans were progressing and the night before Anna-Jane's death, the couple had attended the house of a wedding celebrant and signed the notice to marry.

So they certainly seemed happy on the evening of Friday 18 March 1994 whilst out for after-work drinks at the Norwood Hotel, in Norwood, Adelaide. They had three or four glasses of wine before heading home, arriving about 6:40pm. Anna-Jane called her sister-in-law, Susan Cheney, to finalise pre-arranged plans to walk their dogs. Anna-Jane drove to Susan's house and walked the dogs for 20–30 minutes; Susan later gave evidence to say that Anna-Jane was happy, was not showing signs of being alcohol-affected, and was talking about the coming wedding.

Anna-Jane then drove Susan home, dropping her off between 8pm and 8:05pm, before driving the 8 to 10 minutes back to the home she shared with Henry, arriving around 8:10–8:15pm.

This was the last time that Anna-Jane was seen alive by anyone other than Henry.

Henry Keogh had popped out about 8:15pm to visit his mother, Eileen Keogh, when Anna-Jane had told him she had decided to take a bath. This was corroborated by his mother, who lived around two kilometres from Anna-Jane and Henry's house. She stated in court that her son has arrived at her house around 8:15–8:25pm, leaving at 9:15pm, or maybe a little later.

Henry had returned to the house the couple had shared since late 1991, around 9:30pm, at which point he found Anna-Jane on her side in the bath, with her head under the water, unconscious. He immediately removed her from the bath and tried to resuscitate her.

Keogh said he called the emergency services, and the call was logged by St John Ambulance at 9:32pm. He said, 'My fiancée has had an accident in the bath. I think she drowned.'

Two ambulance staff were on the scene in Adelaide's east at 9:38pm, six minutes after the 000 call came in.

There was no indication of forced entry to the house, or signs of a struggle.

The bath was around three-quarters full of tepid water. Anna-Jane was lying on the floor between the bedroom and the bathroom. Her head was on the carpeted floor of the bedroom, with her feet in the bathroom. Her skin was dry to the touch, but her hair was wet.

The ambulance crew began resuscitation, and immediately expelled water from Anna-Jane's mouth, as well as gastric contents (in other words, Anna-Jane was induced to vomit as a result of the resuscitation attempt). Keogh had stated that he had been trying to resuscitate Anna-Jane since he had found her, but the Crown would later allege that the expulsion of water and gastric contents when the ambulance crew arrived indicated that no previous attempts had been made to save her life.

Sadly, Anna-Jane could not be saved.

At least 10 police officers were quickly in attendance, and they did an evaluation of the scene as would be expected in an unexplained death, taking limited photographs and notes, as well as interviewing Keogh. Henry told them he had come home to find his fiancée completely submerged in the bath. He had lifted her out, placed her on the floor and although he had tried, he had been unable to resuscitate her.

In addition to calling the emergency services, Henry had also called Anna-Jane's parents, Kevin and Joanne Cheney, who had immediately rushed to the couple's home.

In the early stages of the case, the police were not suspicious. This looked like exactly what it later transpired to be, an accidental drowning. Because the police believed this to be an accident the scene was not secured, and as friends and family arrived they were allowed to move around unrestricted and interfere with the death scene.

This included Joanne Chaney cleaning Anna-Jane's face and applying make-up, and Kevin Chaney releasing the water from the bath. This would be considered 'contamination' of a death scene, and is far from good practice on the part of the police to allow this – it removes or alters evidence of what has happened.

The police procedures manual states that with any sudden or unexplained death, the situation must be treated as a potential murder until the cause of death has been determined. This is intended to secure any potential evidence in the event it turns out that a murder has occurred. Normally, even the investigating officers would not be allowed access to the scene until the forensic officers had completed their examination. In this case there was no forensic examination of the scene and no proper photographs were taken. It was just assumed that it was an accidental death.

The Coroner's Constable was then asked to take possession of the body, which was removed shortly after midnight. Anna-Jane was transported to the mortuary so that a post-mortem could be performed – a standard autopsy, with Anna-Jane's death entered into the system as non-suspicious.

EXPERT INSERT: DIFFERENT TYPES OF POST-MORTEMS

A post-mortem (or 'PM', also known as an autopsy) is a highly specialised surgical procedure that consists of both an external and internal examination, including dissection. Autopsies can include the collection of various samples, such as blood and saliva, as well as fingernail clippings. The aim of the examination, which is performed by a medical practitioner who has additional expertise in pathology, is the collection of information relating to cause and manner of death.

There are a number of aims when performing the autopsy, including: to collect information that may assist in determining (if unknown) or confirming the deceased's identity, to establish time since death (a key factor in suspicious deaths), to determine the manner and cause of death, to establish if a death was natural or not, to note the presence and extent of any injuries or diseases, and to retain relevant organs for later examination.

There are different types of post-mortems, depending on the circumstances under which someone died.

When a person has died a natural death and the death was expected (such as those in palliative care), a PM is not normally required. However, if the deceased bequeathed their remains to science, an academic post-mortem may be performed by those studying human anatomy such as medical and dental students for educational purposes.

A 'standard' post-mortem will be carried out in cases of unexpected death, but where there is no suspicion that a crime may have been committed, for example following a fatal fall from a ladder at home. The pathologist will still attempt to confirm cause and manner of death, and will collect samples for processing such as blood, and will note anything suspicious that may have had a bearing on the death. However, they will not run the full range of tests reserved for 'special' or 'forensic' PMs. The purpose of this examination is two-fold – to determine what elements contributed to a person's death, as well as to note any facts that may prevent similar deaths in the future.

Forensic or special post-mortems are performed when a crime is known to have taken place, or there is some suspicion that the death may not have been natural. This is also known as a 'medico-legal' autopsy. During this procedure, the pathologist will attempt to determine not only the cause and manner of death, but also what happened immediately prior to death – for example, if bruises were present on the deceased, is this evidence that there was a struggle? Or where there are a number of cuts to a murder victim's forearms and hands, this indicates they tried to defend themselves from an attacker with a knife. A special PM will collect samples not taken in a standard procedure, and may include biological specimens (including stomach contents) for toxicological analysis, which may indicate whether alcohol, drugs, or poisons are present, together with the quantity; an evaluation can then be made as to what affect these would have had on the deceased, e.g. were drugs identified cut with a particularly toxic substance? As information from forensic

PMs is likely to be used in criminal proceedings, the accuracy of the findings and interpretation of them is critical, as is the possibility of seeking a second opinion if required. Therefore, detailed notes and images, and appropriate samples for later analysis must be taken.

The final type of post-mortem is a 'virtual' or medical imaging PM. This type of autopsy is performed through the use of clinical techniques such as computed tomography (CT), magnetic resonance imaging (MRI), and 3D imaging technologies, but the purpose remains the determination of cause and manner of death. Virtual autopsies can be used as an alternative to a standard examination, although some practitioners would argue they are an insufficient substitute. However, there are many benefits to virtual autopsies, for example, they are a good use of resources as they are less time-consuming, and their application can improve accuracy in determining cause of death over clinical diagnosis in isolation. Undertaking a virtual PM should therefore be considered in situations when an autopsy is not being performed. Virtual PMs are also useful as it is possible to share files internationally, which means second opinions on cause and manner of death can easily be sought from experts around the world. Another benefit of this technology is that these procedures are performed in a virtual space. As a result, where there is significant risk to the pathologist by undertaking a standard autopsy (such as in cases where the deceased may be carrying a highly contagious disease), a virtual PM allows an examination to take place under safe conditions, as there is no physical contact with the body. A further benefit is that some cultures would prefer that standard PMs are not undertaken for religious reasons, and virtual autopsies allow an examination to take place but one that is non-invasive and therefore culturally respectful. The use of magnetic resonance spectroscopy (MRS) in virtual autopsies can also be useful in helping to establish time since death through an analysis of the metabolic concentrations in the tissues.

Upon completion of their examination (whichever form it takes), the pathologist makes a recommendation as to what they think the cause and manner of death were. However, the formal determination is made by a Coroner following a full analysis of all of the facts – including those from the PM, as well as additional information provided by the police and other involved parties such as psychologists, as well as witnesses to events.

The PM was conducted two days later, on 20 March, by Chief Forensic Pathologist Dr Colin Manock, employed at the state's Forensic Science Centre, Adelaide, who also undertook a second examination on 21 March. This is when the case started to take on a different context, as Manock formed a number of opinions that went on to form the basis of the murder charge.

Firstly, he was of the view that the patterns of 'differential staining' (a technique that looks at the proportion of white blood cells in the blood) between the pulmonary artery (which begins in the heart and goes on to divide to deliver deoxygenated blood to the lungs) and the aorta (the main blood vessel carrying blood from the heart to the rest of the body) was a 'classic' sign of drowning (although other researchers have concluded that whilst differential staining may be indicative of freshwater drowning, it should only be used as a corroborative sign and not used in isolation to conclude drowning was the cause of death).

Added to this was the fact that Manock found no sign of trauma to the outer surface of the brain, which he said showed that

Anna-Jane was conscious when her head went under the water in the bath, and that this ruled out that the deceased had slipped and hit her head, before accidentally drowning.

The final evidence Manock used to indicate non-accidental death was that at autopsy he noted what he believed were faint bruises on both the inside and outside of Anna-Jane's calves, the pattern of which indicated to him that someone had gripped her lower legs. Manock was convinced that the three faint bruises on Anna-Jane's left outer calf and single bruise on her inner calf were the result of a hand-grip. Again by extrapolation, Manock then claimed that this showed someone's right hand had grabbed Anna-Jane's leg beneath her calf around the time of death, and that (by another leap of logic) this meant she had been forcibly drowned.

Further bruising was described on the back of her neck and top of her head in the centre of her scalp, which, according to Manock, was the result of her head making contact with the bath as she was forcibly submerged by a second person during a struggle. He said the force necessary to cause these bruises would have been slight, so the trauma was external only, consequently there was no corresponding internal injury.

He looked at the bruises under the microscope, and from the presentation of the tissue, he concluded that they had been caused in the four hours preceding Anna-Jane's death.

Together, as a result of the combination of factors noted during his PM, Manock excluded natural or accident as the cause of death, and instead decided that Anna-Jane's death was suspicious – this was before he had visited the death scene.

This happened a week later, on 27 March, at which point Manock specifically observed the position and dimensions of the bath.

Rather than changing his opinion, his observations at the death scene solidified in his mind that Anna-Jane had been killed.

And he provided an opinion as to how this could have happened, as outlined in his report, filed on 28 June 1994:

> A person sitting at the plug end of the bath could be immersed with relative ease by lifting the feet and at the same time pressing down on the head or on the shoulder with the other hand. This mechanism requires the assailant to place the right hand under the deceased's right ankle and grip the left ankle . . . If the legs are then folded down towards the head the deceased would have been unable to struggle effectively and would quickly lose consciousness . . .
>
> It is my opinion that the bruise at the junction of the neck and the back of the head was caused as the deceased was forced down into the bottom of the bath and represented only a minor blow which would not have caused any loss of consciousness.

Manock said loss of consciousness would have been rapid.

Anna-Jane's blood-alcohol reading did not cause Manock to reconsider his theory of intentional drowning. He felt that 0.1g% was not enough to cause someone to lose consciousness or fall asleep to the point that their head slipping under the water – and the subsequent coughing and spluttering that would result when water hit their vocal cords in association with the resultant burst of adrenalin – would not rouse them.

Manock went on to say that if someone falls or is rendered unconscious by a bang to the head, whilst this may not show externally, there will be evidence of internal trauma at autopsy.

Other pathologists disagreed with this point. A Dr Ross James, also for the Crown and Dr Manock's deputy and successor as South Australia's Chief Forensic Pathologist in 1995, stated that concussion has no defining pathologies, meaning there would not necessarily be physical evidence at PM. However, Dr James did agree with Manock that it was unlikely, with Anna-Jane's blood alcohol concentration (BAC), that she fell asleep and drowned.

Dr James supported Manock's evidence in other ways. He was also not of the opinion that a simple fall had caused the bruising described on her lower legs, or her neck and head.

Needless to say, the defence pathologists did not agree with all of Manock's evidence. Professor Anthony Ansford stated that he could not exclude accident as a cause of death, and that other factors could have contributed – such as epilepsy or myocarditis (inflammation of the heart muscle, which can lead to rapid or abnormal heart rhythms) – even though there was no known history. He did agree that Manock's explanation of the bruising on the left leg was possible.

Another forensic pathologist, Professor Stephen Cordner, gave evidence for the defence. He was very critical of Manock's evidence. Professor Cordner later supplied a report containing his opinions, in which he says that:

> I believe Dr Manock has expressed opinions in this case which are wrong. These wrong views are then combined with other rather speculative propositions to support a reconstruction of this death as a murder. Dr Manock has, in my view, wrongly dismissed an accidental explanation for this death as, at least, a reasonable proposition.
>
> One of my objections to Dr Manock's putting his proposition is that it was not refutable by enquiry or testing and therefore he should have surrounded it with caution. I believe no other forensic pathologist in Australia would be of the view that murder is the only explanation of the findings in this case.

But the forensic evidence wasn't the only cause for concern here. Anna-Jane's family was also suspicious that her death had not been an accident, and made police aware that Anna-Jane had a substantial life insurance policy, with Henry named as the sole beneficiary. Their mistrust ran deeper, and they also insinuated that Keogh was romantically involved with other women. They had therefore offered the police two potential motives – financial and personal; he wanted Anna-Jane out of the way to pursue other women, and to have money to do it in style.

When questioned, Henry not only confirmed the existence of the policy Anna's family knew about, but that there were in fact five separate policies, and he even admitted to having signed them in her name.

To explain this, Keogh stated that, fearing he was going to be laid off from his job, he began working as an agent for five different insurance companies. To keep his position with those companies, he had bought one policy from each in Anna-Jane's name, and forged her signature on the proposals, as well as cheques and debit authorities to cover the premiums. These weren't all secret policies, taken out by Keogh without Anna-Jane's knowledge. At trial the Crown acknowledged that Anna-Jane had known about at least two of them.

Regardless of whether Anna-Jane knew, financial gain represented a strong motive for the prosecution – they alleged Henry stood to gain $1.125 million by cashing in all the policies, but Keogh said the amount he would be eligible to claim would be more like $400,000. Either way, as a divorced father of three children with significant child support responsibilities, money was easily argued as the motivation.

It later transpired that Anna-Jane's family had possibly been right about the other women, as two women came forward independently to say they had had affairs with Keogh when he was living with Anna-Jane.

Both women, known only as witnesses Ms A and Ms B, gave evidence at Keogh's trial. When questioned under oath, Keogh admitted that he had been involved with Ms A, but denied actually having an affair with her. He denied any involvement with Ms B.

At trial, Ms A said she was in a sexual relationship with the accused, beginning in July 1992 and that the relationship continued until December of that year.

Henry and Anna-Jane had become engaged in November of 1992.

Even though Ms A had broken things off with Henry, they began seeing each other again from time to time after December.

According to Ms B, at the same time, Keogh had been in a relationship with her since October 1992. This relationship, according to Ms B, was still going until the week of Anna Jane's death.

The evidence from these women, only some of which Keogh denied, further damaged his credibility in the minds of the jurors. And although it could not be considered evidence of murder, if true, it called into question the true nature of his relationship with Anna-Jane as he could hardly play the part of the devoted, grieving fiancée, who was on the verge of getting married.

The case was hard for the Crown to prove, as all of the evidence was circumstantial – there was no murder weapon or other evidence directly linking Keogh to Anna-Jane's death, and Henry was maintaining his innocence, so no convenient confession either.

The jury in the first trial in 1995 failed to reach a verdict, so a second trial was called.

However, *The Advertiser* newspaper had published an article in error in anticipation of a guilty verdict, referring to Henry's 'tale of treachery'. It was fined $10,000.

Keogh's lawyers then tried to have a permanent stay on any retrial due to the adverse publicity. That application was denied, and the retrial was merely delayed for a short while.

At the second trial, which commenced on 8 August 1995, the Crown asserted that Manock's findings at PM, although circumstantial, were probative of Keogh's guilt. The defence knew this was weak, and accepted that alone the evidence from the PM was not enough to prove guilt beyond reasonable doubt – the criminal legal standard which must be reached in the minds of the jurors before they can return a guilty verdict. However, the Crown argued that when opportunity and motive were added to Manock's evidence, that standard was achieved.

The probative value of Manock's testimony would become a major bone of contention later on, and rightly so given what we know about the terrible flaws in his work, highlighted by the baby death inquiry beginning in 1994.

But Dr Manock was a convincing expert witness. He was apparently highly proficient and a very senior forensic pathologist, having performed around 10,000 post-mortems. And with 30 years' experience as a forensic pathologist, his evidence would have been very persuasive to a jury.

He told the court that he had never been convinced Anna-Jane's death was an accident, as he simply couldn't find an explanation as to why she had drowned.

Why was he so convinced with his theory about the victim being intentionally drowned, and the bruises showing evidence of a hand grip?

At trial, Manock said that as soon as he saw the four 'bruises' on Anna-Jane's calf, and the pattern they formed – to his mind a 'handgrip' – he was reminded of the infamous English case of serial killer and bigamist George Joseph Smith, who had married three times, and each of his new brides had drowned in the bath on their honeymoons. This became known as the 'brides in the bath' (*R v. Smith*) trial when it was heard in 1915. Smith committed his crimes for financial gain, as was the claim against Keogh, between 1912 and 1914, when he forcibly drowned 31-year-old Beatrice Mundy, 25-year-old Alice Burnham, and 38-year-old Margaret Lofty. Smith, who used various aliases, was executed by hanging for his crimes at Maidstone prison on 13 August 1915. It was an important case for forensic pathology, as it was the first to show 'similar fact', i.e. similarities between crimes were used to link them and show deliberation on the part of the accused.

To Manock's eye, he believed Keogh had intentionally drowned his bride-to-be, in the same way that Smith had done over 100 years earlier. Manock seems a little obsessed with this case, as he also mentioned it when giving evidence in the trial of Emily Perry in 1981, when she was accused of attempting to murder her husband with arsenic.

What Manock also failed to acknowledge was that there was a potential reason that Anna-Jane could have drowned by accident – Anna-Jane had been out that evening, and had drunk four or five glasses of wine. At post-mortem her blood-alcohol concentration had come back at 0.1g%, twice the legal driving limit. Anna-Jane weighed 56 kilograms (or 123 pounds), so was a light woman, and a BAC of between 0.08g% and 0.15g% puts you at risk of suffering blurred vision, slurred speech and impaired balance and co-ordination.

Nevertheless, the Crown was insistent that the bruises were the crucial factor, and as Paul Rofe, QC and Director of Public Prosecutions, stated in his summing up at trial, 'If those four bruises on her lower left leg were inflicted at the same time, and that time was just before she died in the bath, there is no other explanation for them, other than a grip. If it was a grip, it must have been the grip of the accused. If it was the grip of the accused, it must have been part of the act of murder.'

I have a few issues with this. Firstly, even if we accept the bruises indicated someone had firmly gripped Anna-Jane's left calf, that in no way proves that Henry was the one who grabbed her. Secondly, even if Henry – or anyone else – had grabbed Anna-Jane, it does not automatically follow that this was during an intentional killing.

This is a fallacy, as the logic is flawed; a bruised calf does not have a cause-effect relationship with deliberate drowning. But argued strongly enough, and by a respected and allegedly highly proficient expert like Manock, how would the jury know differently?

There was also the evidence from the Crown that the lack of gastric expulsion spoke to the fact that Keogh had not tried to resuscitate Anna-Jane. A defence expert, anaesthetist Dr Robert Edwards, said there was no inconsistency between what the ambulance crew reported seeing at the scene and Henry's description of what happened. Edwards stated that around 60cc of water could escape a drowning victim when placed on their side, which could easily soak into a carpet and not be noticed. He also commented that vomiting is a random event, and that in Anna-Jane's case, vomiting was only induced once the ambulance crew used a defibrillator. The scene evidence was therefore consistent with Keogh's version of events. Edwards' evidence with regards to resuscitation was not contradicted by other witnesses.

However, the strong impact of Manock's evidence on the minds of the jurors was further increased when the trial judge for the second trial, in summing up, specifically drew the jury's attention to the doctor's extensive qualifications and experience, leaving it open to them to accept his evidence in its entirety.

This was clearly very significant and had a huge impact on the outcome, and on 23 August 1995, after only five hours of deliberation, the jury unanimously found Keogh guilty of murder. Henry was sentenced to life with a minimum term of 25 years in prison.

As we have pointed out, two days after being convicted, the Coroner released his Findings on the baby deaths, which should have secured the overturning of the conviction on the appeal. However, that failure by the prosecution was not referred to in the Keogh appeal. Keogh's solicitor, Michael Sykes, said:

> I asked Judge David [Keogh's defence lawyer and, by this time, a judge of the District Court of South Australia] if he would make an affidavit deposing to reasons as to why he did not raise in the appeal any issue relating to the Baby Deaths Coronial Findings by the Coroner in relation to Dr Manock. Judge David declined. He informed me that once they were published he had considered them, but could not see how they could assist Keogh. As the Findings only came out after the trial he did not have time to consider them in more than an embryonic level and was without the opportunity for an in-depth analysis prior to the appeal being heard.

The suggestion that the criticisms of Dr Manock contained in the Findings could not assist Keogh is, in my view, frankly astounding. On any view they should have been sufficient for the conviction to be set aside.

There were some three months between the date the Findings were issued and the hearing of the appeal. Surely it would have been possible for an eminent QC such as Mr David to read the 93 pages in that time?

THE LEGAL BATTLE TO FREE KEOGH BEGINS

Following the guilty verdict, Keogh and his legal team launched an appeal to the Court of Criminal Appeal, on the grounds that the evidence of the women who claimed to have had affairs with Keogh should not have been admitted, the trial should have been permanently stayed because of the adverse publicity due to the erroneous newspaper article, and that the verdict of the jury was unreasonable. But on 22 December 1995, this was dismissed.

In December 1996, the first petition was put forward to the Governor of South Australia, which questioned Manock's drowning hypothesis and outlined the criticisms of his evidence in the baby deaths Coronial Findings.

It was denied.

In 1997, Henry applied to reopen the appeal, which was heard by the Supreme Court, on the grounds that the original trial miscarried due to the unavailability of evidence that would establish that Dr Manock's evidence could not be relied on. This request was refused, on the grounds that the court lacked the jurisdiction to hear the appeal.

Keogh's team kept pushing for justice, and applied to the High Court for special leave to appeal in 1997. The court considered two points: 1) that the Coronial Findings should have been considered by the appeal court to overturn the verdict, and the decision of defence counsel not to use that material on the appeal was incompetent; and 2) that the appeal court should have been able to re-open the appeal.

Things got a little complicated at this point, as a further aspect the court had to consider was the fact that the Coroner had also investigated Anna-Jane Cheney's death, and two days after the verdict of guilty against Keogh, had handed very adverse findings against Manock and the adequacy of his post-mortem examination.

Still the High Court refused to grant special leave to appeal the Supreme Court's decision.

In October 2001, the ABC *Four Corners* 'Expert Witness' episode aired, which set out the issues with Dr Manock's qualifications, and his erroneous evidence in Keogh's case and a number of others, including the baby deaths that were subject of the very damning inquiry into Manock's competency as a forensic pathologist. This kind of high profile exposure can help move potential wrongful convictions along, as it draws significant public attention to problems in the criminal justice system.

But in this case, the wheels of justice still continued to turn very slowly.

In 2002, a second petition was lodged with the Governor, specifically outlining the errors and problems with Manock's evidence in Anna-Jane's death. It also drew attention again to Manock's expert opinion in many other cases. Again, this petition was unsuccessful.

In 2003, Keogh's legal team submitted a third petition, stating that the second petition hadn't been considered properly, and criticised both the Attorney General and the Director of Public Prosecutions.

It took another three years, just to get another rejection; in August 2006 the Acting Attorney General, Kevin Foley, said that the complaints raised in the third petition did not present any basis on which the Supreme Court could find a miscarriage of justice had occurred. He had reached this conclusion based on an 'exhaustive report' submitted by the Solicitor General. Foley also stated that there was no deficiency in the prosecution's duty of disclosure.

Mr Foley did not provide reasoning behind his conclusions. Unknown to Keogh and his legal team was the huge irony that Mr Foley's comments raised – at this time, in 2006, the Solicitor General had already obtained advice that stated there was no forensic evidence that Anna-Jane had been murdered.

This was not disclosed until almost nine years later, and would become the basis on which Henry's conviction was finally overturned.

In June 2007, Keogh's team applied again for leave to appeal his conviction to the Supreme Court of South Australia. Another failure.

In November of that year, Henry's legal representatives also again applied for special leave to appeal to the High Court. This was again refused.

On 4 February 2009, Keogh lodged a fourth petition with the Governor of South Australia. The claims now were even more serious: professional misconduct, as this petition was founded on accusations of fraud, deceit, and manifest error on Manock's part. The Governor then passed the petition to the Attorney General of SA for consideration; second appeals can only be granted at the discretion of the Attorney General, and that rarely happens and very few cases were ever heard as a result of the Attorney General referring the case to the Court of Criminal Appeal.

The response to the application to re-open the case via appeal was unanimous: denied.

So the problem was clear – where did that leave those that have been wrongfully convicted, as after one appeal they had exhausted all legal avenues of redress?

At this stage Dr Bob Moles and Associate Professor Bibi Sangha, who had been strong advocates for Henry for many years, sent a complaint to the Australian Human Rights Commission, stating that the criminal appeal system nationwide may have been in breach of international human rights obligations, as it didn't adequately protect the right of the accused to a fair trial and an effective appeal.

Simultaneously, Sangha and Moles had worked with Anne Bressington, a Member of the Legislative Council in SA, to put a Bill to Parliament to establish a Criminal Case Review Commission. This Bill was referred to the Legislative Review Committee, which in July 2012 recommended that a new statutory right of appeal be established.

This was supported by the Attorney General, who accepted that the petition process was inadequate, because it lacked transparency and happened 'behind closed doors'.

So in May 2013, South Australia brought in the *Statutes Amendment (Appeal) Act 2013* (SA), the first such act in the country to allow for a second or subsequent appeal, if there is fresh and compelling evidence that should be heard in the interest of justice; i.e. a miscarriage of justice may have occurred.

Meanwhile, Keogh's legal team had not given up fighting for justice for Henry, but it was only after this new statutory right of appeal was changed in South Australia that allowed for a second appeal.

The tide had finally turned in Henry's favour.

Shortly after lodging his application for leave to appeal, Keogh was provided with a forensic report that had been previously provided to the Solicitor General in 2004 as part of his inquiry into Henry's third petition. This comprised an independent expert opinion by Professor Barrie Vernon-Roberts, the Director of the Forensic Science Centre in Adelaide. This report said that the forensic evidence in Anna-Jane's death did not support the hypothesis that she had been murdered, but rather that her death was likely the result of an accident.

If Professor Vernon-Roberts' report had been divulged when it was submitted, it would have lent further support to Keogh's case. Another failure in disclosure.

Keogh's case was the first to be heard under the newly established right of appeal; fitting, as his case was the stimuli for this issue to be brought to Parliament in the first place.

This was heard in 2014.

The Director of Public Prosecutions kept fighting, and opposed the admission of every item of evidence Keogh's team submitted. He lost on every count. He even opposed the admission of Professor Vernon-Roberts' report, which the Crown had itself obtained in 2004. Again, he was unsuccessful.

Professor Vernon-Roberts was one of a number of experts who

gave evidence at the appeal. After hearing from both sides, the appeal court said the evidence of the expert witnesses was 'compelling' and that the evidence of Dr Manock and his deputy in support of a murder hypothesis amounted to no more than unsubstantiated conjecture; including the now discredited 'grip theory' that was so damaging to Henry's case.

The court concluded that the evidence supporting a homicide as opposed to an accident or medical event was 'largely discredited', and that there was nothing to discount the death as being accidental.

Overall it was found that Dr Manock's evidence had been materially misleading and the autopsy had been incomplete and inadequate. The court determined that there had been a miscarriage of justice due to the flawed expert evidence provided by Dr Manock; specifically, his determination that Anna-Jane had been intentionally drowned, as the Court of Appeal said that the conclusions Manock reached were no more than 'unwarranted speculation'.

The appeal court found that Keogh had been denied a fair trial, and that there had been a substantial miscarriage of justice.

The conviction was overturned, and in December 2014 Henry was released from prison. However, the court was not prepared to enter a verdict of acquittal, and allowed for the DPP to proceed with a retrial.

And proceed they did.

In December 2014, the DPP re-arraigned Keogh for murder, although Keogh was given bail pending retrial, which was set to begin in March 2016.

This was bordering on ridiculous at this stage, as with the forensic pathology evidence being so totally discredited, the prosecution would have to proceed on a purely circumstantial case. Eventually, the Crown saw sense, and in November 2015, at a hearing of the Supreme Court, Adam Kimber from the DPP formally entered a *nolle prosequi* (a formal notice that legal proceedings have been terminated).

You would think that this would have been an end to the matter. Sadly not.

Speculation that Henry had 'got off' on a technicality abounded, as instead of simply accepting that the Crown had no chance of success had they gone forward to trial, they instead opaquely stated that the DPP were not pursuing the case against Keogh because 'a key witness was unable to give evidence at trial'.

The 'key witness' was not named, but was readily accepted to be Manock. Given that his evidence was so thoroughly condemned by this time, it is unfathomable that the Crown would actually have called him.

Instead, Henry was left to deal with the rumours and innuendo that he was guilty of Anna-Jane's murder.

And there are those who still believe Keogh is directly responsible for Anna-Jane's death. In August 2018, the Police Commissioner for SA, Grant Stevens, poured fuel on this fire when he confirmed that Keogh remained a person of interest in Anna-Jane's murder.

And still the Crown won't stop, spurred on in part by Anna-Jane Cheney's family, who remain convinced of Keogh's guilt. In September 2018 they approached the Director of Public Prosecutions to pursue a retrial of Henry for her murder, as they believe this is the only way they will achieve 'closure' on the matter.

In November 2018, however, the Attorney General for South Australia, Vickie Chapman, announced that the SA Government was paying Keogh $2.57 million in compensation after he spent almost 20 years in prison, arising as a result of a miscarriage of justice. This ex-gratia (meaning this was done out of a sense of moral rather than legal obligation) payment was made in order to avoid civil litigation – but Keogh was not impressed. Having originally asked for $6 million, Henry did not feel $2.57 million made up for the 19 years he had spent in prison.

Ms Cheney's family were outraged when this news was released, as they had not been consulted, and were confused as to why someone would be paid compensation when they had not been acquitted.

This led to intense media speculation about the justice of the award of compensation, as Keogh was still being referred to as a murder suspect and Anna-Jane as a murder victim, despite the undisputed forensic evidence at Keogh's retrial that showed her death was almost certainly the result of a slip-and-fall accident.

It sounds contradictory, but it would have been in Henry's favour to go forward to trial, as ultimately he would have been acquitted, and that would have been the line that needed to be drawn under this awful mess.

WHAT WENT WRONG?

The short answer is many things. For example, Keogh's defence team did a poor job at the original trial, as much of the evidence admitted against Henry was highly prejudicial and should not have been heard by the jury.

But the longer answer is Dr Manock.

Manock retired shortly after Keogh was found guilty in 1995, having completed 10,000 post-mortems and provided countless expert opinions in thousands of cases.

But does that make his evidence reliable?

Clearly not.

Law Professor Bob Moles, who read the transcripts from the Keogh case, didn't think so, and immediately recognised that there were problems with the pathologist's evidence.

For example, during the trial Dr Manock was handed a black and white image of Anna-Jane's left calf, and asked to highlight the areas that he believed showed bruising before the jury saw it. No full-length image was produced. What should have happened is that the jury should have been shown the images and been allowed to decide for themselves if there was any bruising present.

A decent defence would have objected on the basis that this was leading the jury, and was prejudicial against the accused.

Moles became more and more interested in the evidence given by Manock, not just in the Keogh case, but over a dozen others in which the pathologist had given expert testimony.

In 2002, Henry had lodged a complaint with the Medical Board of South Australia, the basis of which was that Manock's forensic post-mortem of Anna-Jane had been performed negligently, and worse, that his work on the case, including the opinions he presented at trial as to the cause of death, was not scientifically based, and that this amounted to professional misconduct.

EXPERT INSERT: THE RESPONSIBILITIES OF EXPERTS IN CRIMINAL TRIALS

Normally, a witness may only give evidence as to facts which are the product of their experience. To refer to a ring on someone's finger as 'yellow metal' may be a fact. To refer to it as a 'gold' ring may involve the expression of an opinion. However, a person who has acquired 'specialist knowledge' through study or training (an expert) may be allowed to give opinion evidence, but only if it is necessary to assist jurors in understanding the evidence in a case. For example, a juror may need expert assistance to understand the effect of unfamiliar drugs on a person. They are unlikely to require expert assistance to help them understand that people who consume alcohol may become inebriated.

The general requirements are as follows:

1. Expert evidence presented to the court should be, and should be seen to be, the independent product of the expert uninfluenced as to form or content by the exigencies of litigation.
2. An expert witness should provide independent assistance to the court by way of objective, unbiased opinion in relation to matters within their expertise. An expert witness should never assume the role of an advocate.
3. An expert witness should state the facts or assumptions upon which the opinion is based and should not omit to consider material facts which could detract from the concluded opinion.
4. An expert witness should make it clear when a particular question or issue falls outside their expertise.
5. If an expert's opinion is not properly researched because there is insufficient data available, then this must be stated with an indication that the opinion is no more than a provisional one. In cases where an expert witness who has prepared a report could not assert that the report contained the truth, the whole truth and nothing but the truth without some qualification, that qualification should be stated in the report.
6. If, after exchange of reports, an expert witness changes their view on a material matter, having read the other side's expert's report or for any other reason, such change of view should be communicated (through legal representatives) to the other side without delay and when appropriate to the court.

7. Where expert evidence refers to photographs, plans, calculations, analyses, measurements, survey reports or other similar documents, these must be provided to the opposite party at the same time as the exchange of reports.

This list has been influential in terms of the development of rules of court and upon further court judgments. The underlying need is for 'proper and full disclosure to all parties' so that the opinion can be properly tested in court.

It is important to ensure that it is not only the factual assumptions which are proved, but also the reasoning process which links them to the conclusion.

Experts are also sometimes selected because they have given similar evidence in past cases, and lawyers will go through lists of experts until they arrive at the most favourable one that will give evidence to suit their purpose. Some experts make whole careers out of acting as experts, and become known for postulating specific opinions; these opinions won't vary regardless of the facts of the case.

And some offer misleading or even fabricated evidence to help secure convictions. Others simply cut corners. And the implications are huge.

An infamous example is Laurence Webb, until 2016 one of Western Australia's leading forensic biologists, who worked as a senior DNA analyst for PathWest Laboratory Medicine, an NATA (National Association of Testing Authorities) accredited, state-run pathology centre in WA for 15 years. Webb undertook analyses, prepared reports and gave expert evidence in dozens of cases. However, what people didn't know was that Webb was failing to follow standard protocols, and neglected to have his work independently verified by his peers – a requirement before certificates of analysis were issued so that evidence could be presented in court. Webb was sacked for his misconduct in 2017.

Webb's involvement cast doubt on at least 19 cases involving 27 criminal convictions, achieved between 2008 and 2014. Each of the convicted persons had been contacted, and some may have had grounds to challenge their convictions. One of the high profile cases that this debacle affected was that of convicted murderer Cameron Mansell, as Webb gave evidence at his trial – a case that hinged on a combination of DNA and circumstantial evidence. Prosecutors alleged that Craig Puddy, a millionaire businessman, confronted Mansell at Puddy's home, after Puddy alleged Mansell had stolen money from a bar owned by Puddy, at which Mansell worked. Mansell instead claimed three men arrived at the house when he was there and argued with Puddy over a drug debt, before they killed him, and framed Mansell for the murder. Mansell was handed a life sentence in 2011, with a minimum term of 18 years without parole, after being found guilty of murdering Puddy, who police alleged died at his home in Mount Pleasant, south Perth, although his body has never been found. Mansell has always maintained his innocence, and is considering appealing his conviction now Webb's mishandling of cases has come to light.

Western Australia's Attorney General, John Quigley, described the mess as an 'unprecedented disaster' that would have significant consequences, and that 'this is as serious as it gets in the administration of criminal justice'. Quigley also claimed that on more than one occasion PathWest urged the

Department of Public Prosecutions to not make any disclosures about the breaches in protocol – a clear attempt to protect its reputation at the expense of justice.

Dr Bob Moles, lawyer and expert in miscarriages of justice

And in my view there certainly were problems with Manock's evidential collection procedures during the post-mortem and the report that was produced as a result.

For example, it never became clear as to whether colour photographs were taken of Anna-Jane's body, but the black and white images that were presented in court were of a poor quality. This made it particularly challenging for the jury to be able to determine if any bruising was even present on Anna-Jane's calf, and even more prejudicial given that Manock literally circled areas he claimed were bruises. How could the jury make a balanced decision based on that evidence?

There were also few histological samples taken for later evaluation, and Manock did not maintain his notes – and those that did survive were brief. This lack of adequate sample and data retention became even more problematic given the fact that Anna-Jane's body was released the very same day her case was upgraded to a murder inquiry, so the possibility of collection of more samples that would be required to assist the criminal process became impossible.

But there were even problems with the way the Medical Board approached its review of Keogh's complaint. The Board was primarily concerned that Henry would use the proceedings to upset his conviction.

That was true, it was part of Henry's agenda – but why shouldn't it be? If he could demonstrate that Manock's evidence was inherently unreliable, that should raise doubts over his conviction.

So this is a legitimate aim.

As it turned out, Manock made a number of retractions before the Board in relation to evidence he had given at Keogh's trial; for example, Manock changed his mind as to whether the 'grip-mark' on Anna-Jane was made by a left or a right hand.

These recantations later became part of the basis for Henry's conviction being overturned.

But that was almost 20 years later, years Keogh would spend in prison.

Three pathologists, who made up the majority of the Board members, all agreed that Manock's conduct had been unprofessional – as evidenced through internal memoranda that was circulated to the rest of the panel.

One of the communications about the case was submitted by one of the pathologists on the panel, a Dr Coleman, during the deliberations. When setting out his views of the case, Dr Coleman described the post-mortem procedure performed by Manock on Anna-Jane as 'sub-standard', and his record of the procedure as 'deficient in detail and substance'.

Dr Coleman went on to write that:

The conclusions drawn by Dr Manock, even if reasonable and even if correct went beyond the available evidence which did not appear to allow exclusion of alternative diagnoses and did not explore potential natural antecedents to drowning . . . I agree with Ian Maddocks' [another pathologist on the Board] conclusion that Dr Manock merits reprimand and exclusion from further independent function as a forensic pathologist. If one takes this view then the charge of unprofessional conduct is proven.

Damning.

However, when the final decision was handed down, the Board unanimously determined that unprofessional conduct had not been established and the complaint was dismissed.

But that didn't mean Keogh's team was going to give up.

In 2006, Keogh's legal team applied for judicial review of the Medical Board's decision, and in 2007, the Medical Board's decision was overturned by the Supreme Court.

The matter was referred back to the Medical Board for reconsideration, who now flipped position and supported the view that Manock had in fact been guilty of unprofessional conduct. The Medical Board then took over the complaint, and in 2008 took it before the Medical Tribunal, alleging Manock had been guilty of incompetence and negligence whilst performing the post-mortem on Anna-Jane.

In late 2009, the Tribunal handed down its decision – it found the complaint against Manock had not been substantiated.

But clearly, by this time, Henry's legal team had developed a number of significant concerns with Manock's evidence.

The bruise: this had now become really contentious. Manock admitted during the Medical Tribunal hearing when he was investigated for serious professional misconduct that there was a problem with the tissue samples he had taken to demonstrate the patches of dark skin he noticed at autopsy were in fact bruises. When analysed, the 'thumb' print from the marks he hypothesised indicated Anna-Jane's calf had been 'grabbed' came back negative as being a bruise. This means there was no evidence that this was a bruise at all. Manock knew this at the time of the trials, and still maintained it was evidence of intentional harm.

But this revelation was not as stunning as when Manock, when being interviewed for *60 Minutes* in 2011, stated that the bruises (which he still maintained the marks were) could have been made three or four days before death – not shortly before death 'and certainly no more' than four hours before Anna-Jane drowned, as he had stated in his evidence at trial. Given that the bruise was presented as evidence of a 'grip', and that that was described by Mr Rofe for the Crown as 'the one positive indication of murder', it was unbelievable that Manock was now directly contradicting himself and undermining the evidence he had given at trial.

Drowning as a cause of death: after reviewing images of the scene, the question was being raised as to whether there was even enough water in the bath when Anna-Jane died to facilitate intentional drowning in the manner described by Manock. Was the conclusion by Manock feasible?

Other possibilities besides murder: at the Tribunal into Manock's alleged professional misconduct, he also admitted that it would have been possible for Anna-Jane to lose consciousness in the bath following a fall which would leave no evidence of trauma on the brain. Again, this directly contradicted what he had said at trial, and suggested he had failed to consider any possibilities other than intentional drowning as the cause of death.

Surely, as Manock was the key Crown witness, this 'recantation' in front of the Medical Board was enough to warrant Keogh's conviction to be overturned.

Sadly, this did not happen. Well, not yet.

What had become clear was that all of Manock's work needed reviewing. You would think that someone in his position was an expert – suitably qualified to be undertaking a highly specialised role.

Frighteningly, you'd be wrong.

Manock was not an expert in forensic pathology. And he had no training in histology (the study of tissues using a microscope) – a requisite for a forensic pathologist – the skill he would have needed to determine the marks were, in fact, bruises when viewed through a microscope.

He was appointed as SA's chief forensic pathologist in 1968, even though he had no formal qualifications in pathology. He was employed by the Institute of Medical and Veterinary Science (which later became the state's Forensic Science Centre), who would later admit that they employed Manock as they were desperate, even though they knew he was totally unsuitable for the position.

The problem was compounded when Manock was exempted from having to do the five years of study or sitting the written exams normally required to join the Royal College of Pathologists of Australia – ironic, as on their website it says 'Pathology gives life's most important answers'.

Generally true, but not in Manock's case.

So let's look at these bruises, which were so impactful in this case.

As we have seen, Manock determined that a number of marks on Anna-Jane's body were bruises. The only way to confirm this is to look at the marks under the microscope.

Manock removed some tissue from the deceased's inner left calf, the mark he believed represented the thumb of a hand grip.

This tissue was then independently analysed by Dr Tony Thomas, who concluded that the tissue showed no sign of bruising.

Without the 'thumb' bruise, the whole notion that Anna-Jane's leg had been forcibly gripped to intentionally drown her is undermined. And remember, in Keogh's trial, the Crown had argued that the grip was 'the one positive indication of murder'. And the grip bruise equalling murder scenario was further undermined by pathologist Dr Thomas' evaluation.

According to an affidavit Dr Thomas submitted to the Medical Board of South Australia and to the Solicitor General, Manock had excised a section of only one of the 'finger bruises' for analysis. When analysed histologically, Dr Thomas concluded that there was evidence of bruising, however, it could have been acquired any time within 24 hours prior to death, or immediately after death. He went on to add that, due to its presentation, the bruise may have actually been caused through the removal of tissue during autopsy, and in that way was not a bruise as defined by Manock, but a post-mortem artefact.

IN THE END . . .

If we discount, as we now must, Manock's assertion that Anna-Jane had been gripped around her calves and intentionally drowned, there is literally no evidence to suggest Henry had anything to do with her death. He lost almost 20 years of his life.

Consequently, his wrongful conviction is a miscarriage of justice.

The continued harassment by the DPP is a secondary insult to a man that has already suffered so much at the hands of our legal system.

But Keogh is not the only one who suffered a miscarriage of justice as a result of Manock's expert evidence. Families of Manock's other cases are still seeking justice, decades after their loved ones died.

In August 2018, Joshua Nottle's mum, Julie-Ann Pope, spoke on the 25th anniversary of her son's death. Joshua's case was one of the ones reviewed as part of the baby deaths inquiry in 1994–1995, following the flawed expert testimony provided by Manock in those sad deaths. Ms Pope called for a Royal Commission into the handling of cases, such as Joshua's, by disgraced forensic pathologist Colin Manock.

The ripples of Manock's unprofessionalism and lack of training will be felt for a very long time, and my heart goes out to the families of all those affected.

FIVE

KHALID BAKER:
FIGHTING TO CLEAR HIS NAME
(2005)

'When you know you are innocent you will fight
to the day you die'
Khalid Baker, talking to *60 Minutes* in October 2019

In the early hours of 27 November 2005, a party was in full swing in a converted warehouse in Melbourne. Up to 200 people were having fun, there was a great atmosphere, with music and dancing, people dressed to theme – a roller-disco. But things changed. What started in fun ended with 22-year-old Albert Snowball dead, and 18-year-old Khalid Baker being found guilty of his murder and sentenced to 17 years in prison.

I am good friends with one of Khalid's staunchest supporters, Dr Michele Ruyters, from RMIT University's Bridge of Hope Innocence Initiative. Michele has been fighting for justice for Khalid for a number of years, and I became fascinated by a young man who has been through so much, but has shown such strength in the face of serious adversity. I've followed his story, and whilst shocked by what happened to him, I was inspired by his determination and courage. This is a story everyone should hear.

To set the scene, Khalid has always maintained his innocence. That is not unusual for convicted killers. But the twist in this case is that Khalid's childhood friend (known by the pseudonym LM, as he was only 17 years old at the time of the incident) has openly admitted to being the last person to touch Albert, pushing him away to end an altercation before Snowball fell to his death. LM agreed that pushing Albert was wrong, but claimed it all happened in the heat of a fight, and that far from trying to hurt Snowball, he was actually trying to stop the fight; in essence he was acting as the peacekeeper.

This was just an awful accident.

But in court, LM was acquitted, whilst Khalid was found guilty of murder.

And LM feels the burden of that not guilty verdict every day.

For many people, being found guilty would have been the end. Many people give up, even when they are innocent, as hope in prison can be dangerous; it can be the thing that breaks you.

But not Khalid. He is, by his very nature, a fighter.

Born on 10 July 1987 in Saudi Arabia to Ethiopian parents, five-year-old Khalid and his family migrated to Australia from Somalia in 1992. With three older siblings, Khalid is the fourth of six children, with the youngest, Urgi, born in Australia. The family originally lived in Sydney, before moving to Melbourne.

Life was not smooth for the family. Khalid did not get on with his parents and siblings, which led to him living out of a suitcase from ages 12 to 14, at which point he went back to live at home.

Khalid was also struggling to fit in at school, and because he had difficulty learning to read and write, he was bullied. He suffered racial abuse, and was ridiculed and embarrassed by his fellow students, which led to him being expelled in 2002, aged 14 years.

When he was 15, Khalid turned to boxing, and his talent soon shone. He won the title of junior lightweight champion of Australia. This really put the fire to succeed into Baker.

Simultaneous to gaining prominence in the ring though, Khalid was also drawing the attention of the police. He was charged with several criminal offences between 2001 and 2005, including one charge of recklessly causing injury, resisting arrest, one charge of burglary, and one of wilful damage. But although he was found guilty of all of these charges, he had never been to prison.

But none of this history supported that Khalid would intend to cause someone serious injury sufficient to kill.

A young man with a bright sporting future, cut short by a murder conviction.

Khalid has always denied harming Albert; 2019 saw him released on parole after 13 years in prison, but that is not enough for Baker. He wants to clear his name.

He is in the fight of his life, and he has some heavy hitters on his side – RMIT University's Bridge of Hope Innocence Initiative has taken on his case, and Dr Michele Ruyters, Director of the initiative, firmly believes he could not have pushed the victim to his death and that his conviction should be overturned. A petition for mercy has been made to the Attorney General in Victoria, and, as I write, Khalid's supporters are nervously awaiting the result.

The media has also rallied behind him after I contacted Ali Langdon, a journalist and true crime writer from Channel Nine's *60 Minutes*, who I have worked with before. Ali agreed the case warranted investigation, and the result was a special on Khalid called 'Fight of his Life', which aired in October 2019.

I do believe, as do many others, that Khalid Baker did not have anything to do with the death of Albert Snowball. There is evidence, as you will see, that he was nowhere near him when he crashed through the window and fell to his death.

But still he went to prison for murder.

As we go through this case, we will face an uncomfortable truth, that the outcome may have been influenced by the race of the witnesses that gave evidence in court, the white witnesses identified Khalid as the man who pushed the victim, and ultimately they were believed over the black witnesses who said LM was the person fighting with Albert.

But the truth is not black and white, it is a murky shade of grey with these competing and contradictory accounts of what 'really' happened.

What is clear to me is that this is a miscarriage of justice, as the evidence does not support guilty beyond reasonable doubt, and a young man lost 13 years of his life.

So this is a story of tragedy, of injustice, of suffering. But it is also a story of hope, of an inspirational man fighting the odds, who is full of forgiveness and positivity, rather than anger and bitterness. Khalid Baker is an inspiration to everyone facing adversity.

If anyone can win and get justice, it's Khalid.

THE CASE

As with many tragedies, the situation that led to 22-year-old Albert Snowball's death was unpredictable and started in fun. Mix hundreds of young partygoers with alcohol and racial tension, and you have a recipe for disaster.

The night had been going well, a roller-disco-themed party in a converted warehouse in Brunswick, an inner-city suburb of Melbourne known for its strong live music and arts scene. This was a housewarming and a birthday party combined, and people were having fun.

A group of friends, Khalid Baker amongst them, had arrived at the party around midnight. Khalid was the designated driver, and was only there as he had driven LM and three other friends, Ali Faulkner, Lado Morgan, and Nassir Asfer, to the party because LM had been invited to perform a few songs live with the band, and as an aspiring hip hop musician this was a big break for him – his first live performance.

About 3am on Sunday 27 November 2005, Khalid and another friend were dancing, having a laugh. But one of their group, Ali Faulkner, had got drunk and aggressive. He started a fight on the dance floor, and being his friends, Khalid and LM went to try to disentangle Faulkner from the brawl.

That's when things turned nasty.

The three young men – Faulkner, Khalid, and LM – were facing a pack of about 100 people, all wanting to fight them. Khalid and LM were trying to break the fight up, but when people started throwing punches and kicking out, they knew they had to fight back as they were seriously outnumbered.

Khalid was sober and clear-headed. All he wanted to do was get out of there. When he talks about that night, he describes how threatened he felt facing such a large group, and of throwing a wine bottle to clear a path. And he did kick out, but this was all done, according to Khalid, in self-defence.

Khalid was not the aggressor, as the court documents would have you believe, which state that Khalid was involved in an outburst of 'unprovoked violence' and that 'Baker and Faulkner attacked party-goers at random and inflicted injuries'.

The aggressor was actually Faulkner, who was later charged and pleaded guilty to a number of assault-related offences, and was subsequently sentenced to five years and nine months in prison, with a minimum non-parole period of four years.

Regardless, Khalid was fighting grown men. But it is likely none of those men were champion boxers like Baker.

Khalid, LM, and Faulkner managed to get out into a stairwell on the second floor, which had a set of stairs leading down to the first floor with a landing half-way down, railings overlooking the stairs, and an almost full-length window looking down to the pavement below.

Khalid and Faulkner were on their way down the stairs to leave by the exit door below, and LM was not far behind them.

Albert Snowball and a bunch of others from the party followed them out into the stairway via the doorway on the second floor to continue the argument.

Khalid then says that Snowball started making racial slurs, and both Khalid and LM started back up the stairs. LM made it to the top, but Khalid was restrained before he got to the top step. He picked up a chair, as his childhood friend, LM, was fighting with Albert on the landing upstairs. But the chair was taken off Khalid, and he was pushed back down the stairs.

LM says that he and Albert were throwing punches, none connecting, and LM pushed Snowball backwards, to get some distance between them, LM estimates about 1.5 metres. He then turned his back and went down the stairs.

Meanwhile, Khalid was now also heading downstairs, and says by the time he reached the bottom near the exit door, he could see someone lying on the pavement outside.

That was Albert Snowball, having fallen 5.4 metres through the window upstairs to the footpath below, hitting his head on the pavement. He was rushed to Royal Melbourne Hospital in a critical condition and suffering severe brain damage from the fracture to his skull, but died two days later as a result of the injuries he sustained.

THE EVIDENCE

This is where things get a little messy.

Some witnesses at the party claim to have seen Khalid push Albert, others say LM was the one fighting with Snowball. And LM was not hiding his involvement in what happened. He admitted his part in the fight that led to Albert's fall in his very first police interview the night of the incident, saying, 'I grabbed him and pushed him. I turned around and kept walking. By the time I got downstairs, the guy was on – on the pavement . . . I – I think he fell through the window.'

Over 14 years later he has continued to maintain he was responsible, as he was the last person fighting with Snowball; though LM never actually saw Albert go through the window as he had turned away by that point, and isn't sure if his push was what caused Albert to fall. So he does not feel guilty of murder, as there was never any intent on his part to seriously injure Snowball.

Still, he knows Khalid had nothing to do with it.

LM's story has not changed at all in the intervening years. He maintained his position throughout the court case and still in 2019, when he was interviewed by Ali Langdon for the *60 Minutes* special that threw light on Khalid's fight for justice.

LM made it very clear to police in an interview that was recorded that Khalid wasn't even on the landing at the time that Albert fell. This supports Khalid's description of events, that he was part way down the stairs, blocked from getting involved in the scuffle by other partygoers, a number of whose evidence we will review shortly.

Neither Khalid or LM gave evidence at trial, but three witnesses who were there back-up this version of events.

LM kept telling the police Khalid wasn't even near the victim. They just won't believe him.

There was no forensic evidence linking Khalid to Albert's fall, but the police pursued the case anyway, and Khalid and LM were jointly charged with Snowball's murder. They were tried separately, with the case against each also considered independently, but at the same time, in the Supreme Court of Victoria, as the Crown contended they were acting in concert in assaulting the victim.

As there was no actual evidence, when the case got to court the jury was left relying solely on witness accounts of what happened.

But the witness accounts, as we have seen, are contradictory – in fact no two accounts are the same – which is not at all surprising given the circumstances. Remember, it was an intense few minutes, there were lots of people moving around in a small, dark space, over a short period of time, many of whom were drunk.

And no one actually saw Snowball go through the window.

There were six eyewitnesses who gave evidence as to what happened on the stairwell, in the moments leading up to Snowball's fall through the window. They all agreed on one thing – that a fight broke out on the top floor landing, and that someone fell through the window. What they didn't agree on was who was fighting whom, and how the victim fell – or was pushed – through the window. The witnesses split into two, distinct groups – those who stated Baker was the man fighting with Albert, and those who thought LM was the man involved. Three of the six implicated Khalid.

But their accounts did not correspond and varied at times, leading to questions as to their reliability. One witness, Asher Doig, said five or six men came out of the exit door at the top of the landing and headed down the stairs, whereas Peter Arcaro (another witness who had been next to Doig on the landing) said three or four African men came onto the landing, walked past him and went down to the middle landing.

Doig also gave evidence to say that Khalid 'king hit' Snowball but under cross-examination, whilst denying his recollection was shaky, accepted that he could be mistaken in his recollection of what happened.

There were more inconsistencies between these two witnesses as to how many were involved in the fight itself – Doig said two men were simultaneously attacking Snowball, whereas Arcaro said it was a one-on-one fight, and that Doig had tried to restrain Khalid. Arcaro, under cross-examination, rejected the suggestion that LM had come onto the landing and started fighting with the victim.

Earl Stuart's evidence, the third witness who implicated Khalid, was different again. He said three African men (we can assume Baker, LM, and Morgan, as Faulkner is of Arabic or Lebanese appearance) were ushered out of the exit door by others, and he described Khalid as the most agitated at having been removed from the party. The men started down the stairs, but then came back up to resume fighting with others at the top of the stairs on the landing. Stuart said that whilst there was a frenzy of fighting, and it was severe in intensity, the victim fell through the window as a result of being 'pushed back by the force of what was occurring', and that Baker went into a 'furious rage'. Under cross-examination, however, Stuart said that the man Khalid was fighting was not the person who fell through the window – this was a direct contradiction to what he had said when questioned by the Crown. The prosecutor attempted to undo some of the damage done to his case in closing, when he described Stuart as a 'fairly odd sort of individual', and that he had given 'some very odd evidence'. If by odd he means conflicting, well yes, but as one of the prosecution's own witnesses was not sure Baker was the man fighting with Snowball, this should have raised some doubts, given the inconsistencies in the other eyewitnesses' identification evidence for the Crown.

Let's look at the alternative version of events, as expressed by three other witnesses – Nassir Asfer and Lado Morgan, who were friends of Baker's and had gone to the party with him, and Eric Masonga, who was also of African origin, but did not know Khalid.

Asfer's evidence most closely corresponds to Khalid's, as both men say that Baker and Faulkner left the party room first and began to head down the stairs. According to Asfer, they looked upset and told him they had been involved in a fight inside the party.

Snowball then followed them out and asked why they had hit him. Khalid and Faulkner had started to walk downstairs, but then started back up the stairs, just as LM came out onto the landing. Asfer then says he grabbed Baker, and Morgan held Faulkner, to stop them getting involved in any more trouble; as a result, if we believe Asfer's version, Baker could not have pushed Snowball, as Asfer was personally restraining him at the top of the stairs, although Khalid was trying to free himself from Asfer's grasp. He said that he saw LM and Albert punching each other, with Snowball facing the stairs and LM the window. Asfer then heard the window break, but did not see it, as he was still tussling with Khalid.

Asfer also gave evidence as to LM's statement in the car, which would later be classed as an additional admission, when he was arguing with Faulkner and said, 'Look what you made me do.' This indicates LM blamed Faulkner for the fight, not Baker. This was also witnessed by Khalid and Morgan.

Lado Morgan, the final of the friends on the landing, said he had not seen the fight inside the party, but did see Khalid and Faulkner come into the stairwell and head down to the first landing. Then he agrees with the other accounts that state that Snowball then came onto the top landing and started the argument again. Morgan then says Baker and Faulkner headed back upstairs, at which point LM came through the exit onto the landing as well. Morgan then held Faulkner back, as he knew there was going to be a fight, and Asfer restrained Khalid (a key point both Lado and Asfer agree on). Another core point is that Morgan saw LM fighting with Snowball, and Khalid wasn't fighting anyone. Morgan also witnessed the comment in the car by LM, and made reference to it in his police statement.

Eric Masonga's version varies slightly from Asfer's and Morgan's. Masonga says he saw Khalid, Faulkner, and LM come out onto the landing and head downstairs to the middle landing. Then Baker and LM came back to the top landing, where Khalid began fighting with one white male, and LM fought with another white male – Snowball. So, according to Masonga, there were two separate fights taking place at the top of the stairs, but either way he never saw Baker fighting the victim. Initially, in his evidence in chief, Masonga said he had not seen Albert fall, but under cross-examination, he said that Snowball was fighting with LM, but had lost his balance so he took no more than two steps backwards to recover it and fell out of the window. He was clear that LM was the last person to have any physical contact with the victim before he fell. Unfortunately, Masonga was not considered a reliable witness, as when he had first been questioned by the police, he said he hadn't seen any fight on the landing. He had to explain this in court, as he was forced to acknowledge that his first state-ment included a number of 'inventions'. He said he had made and signed this false statement as he had not wanted to get involved; he didn't know either of the accused personally, so why get caught up in their mess?

In court, the prosecution broke the witnesses down simply into two groups – black and white. And whatever way we look at it, race has a big impact on this case.

The versions presented by the witnesses are not reconcilable – according to the white witnesses on the landing (Doig, Arcaro, and

Stuart), Khalid was the person who was fighting with Snowball, essentially exonerating LM of any blame.

The black witnesses (Asfer, Morgan, and Masonga) identified LM as the person fighting with Snowball, and confirmed Khalid was either being physically restrained at the time or was fighting someone else entirely, thereby effectively exonerating Baker. These last witnesses confirm LM's own statement, that he was the last person to touch Snowball before he fell.

We should remember that Khalid and his friends were unknown to the white witnesses, as they had never met before the party, whereas the witnesses who say Baker was not the one fighting with Snowball could be argued to be more reliable as they were Khalid's friends (except Masonga) and are more likely to notice where Baker and LM were during the fight.

Nevertheless, the white witnesses must have been more believable to the jury, as they convicted Khalid. They were articulate when giving evidence, and clearly understood the process of how evidence should be given. But this does not make them inherently more reliable as witnesses, or their evidence more truthful than the other witnesses'.

I am not suggesting for one moment the white witnesses were lying in their evidence, they may have genuinely thought they were correct – perhaps in the dark, in that crowded space, with things moving quickly in a violent and heated exchange, they simply couldn't tell one guy apart from the other, as we know that witnesses are bad at correctly identifying people outside of their own racial group; relevant as Baker, LM, and Morgan are all Ethiopian Australians, and Faulkner is of Arabic or Lebanese appearance.

But they told a better story, and one the jury found more compelling. Without any forensic evidence, that's all it took to see a young man found guilty of murder.

That is what Khalid believed happened, saying, 'When, say, a white person sees an Asian and [says] they all look alike, they can't really tell the difference, it was like that with the white witnesses.'

And we know eyewitnesses make mistakes all the time.

EXPERT INSERT: WITNESS MISIDENTIFICATION BASED ON RACE

There are two possible reasons why Khalid was falsely identified by the Caucasian witnesses and not by the black witnesses. Firstly is a psychological phenomenon called the 'own-race bias' or 'cross race effect'. There is a tendency for us to be much better at recognising people who are the same race as us and less accurate at identifying people who are of a different race. The own-race bias has serious ramifications for eyewitness evidence, especially as research has shown that people are more likely to make a false identification of an innocent suspect if they are a different race to them. Furthermore, eyewitness identification is powerful evidence for convictions even though it has been shown to be unreliable. As many as 75 per cent of false convictions have resulted from incorrect identifications and of these the majority were from witnesses identifying a suspect of a different race to themselves. Many of these misidentifications have since been overturned by DNA evidence, which has shown the suspects to be innocent, but often after serving long jail sentences.

The best current explanation for own-race bias is the 'contact hypothesis', that through everyday contact we become experts at identifying people who are the same race as us, and less accurate with people who are of a different race. However, this often depends on the demographics of the country we live in so, for example, in countries where the majority of the people are Caucasian, then Caucasians will probably show an own-race bias and be less accurate at recognising people who aren't Caucasian, but people from different ethnicities might not exhibit an own-race bias, as they have lots of contact with Caucasians, and gain experience in recognising their faces. For example, Chinese people in Australia may be equally good at telling Caucasian and Chinese faces apart, as they see both all the time. So long-term exposure is the key to accurate identification and differentiation, known as a 'experience-dependent perceptual phenomenon'. This affect can be exacerbated under noisy and uncertain conditions, such as those often associated with criminal activity.

Another reason why Khalid may have been misidentified as the culprit relates to another psychological phenomenon called 'unconscious transference'. This is when a witness sees a crime and then later recognises someone from the scene of the crime, but mistakes an innocent bystander they've seen before as the perpetrator of the crime. One explanation for why a witness would identify an innocent person who they had seen somewhere else, is that when the witness recognises the person, they forget the context, that is they misremember the bystander as being the culprit. This happens without the witness's knowledge, i.e. unconsciously. It might be that the witness's memory of Khalid was unconsciously transferred, so that he was misremembered as being the culprit of the crime, rather than a bystander. The unconscious transfer of the memory may have also been further influenced by Khalid being a different race to some of the witnesses, as research has shown that people are more likely to identify innocent other-race people through unconscious transferences, as compared to same-race individuals – a combination of effects leading to a misidentification.

Misidentification based on race is not, sadly, a new phenomenon. In 1975, a man broke into two houses in Franklin County, Ohio, in the US and raped two white women; the perpetrator became known as the 'Grandview Rapist', due to the Columbus neighbourhood where the early attacks took place. In January 1978, William Bernard Jackson, a young father, was convicted by a jury of two counts of rape and sentenced to between 14 and 50 years in prison. The only evidence against him was the eyewitness identification of his victims, who both swore under oath that William was the man who had raped them. But they were wrong.

In 1983, a prominent Columbus physician, Dr Edward Jackson (no relation to William), was arrested on aggravated burglary charges. He had been caught in the home of two women, who thankfully weren't in, with a bag containing rope, surgical gloves, and a ski mask – these items had all been used by the Grandview Rapist. When the police undertook a search of Edward Jackson's home, they found a list of his rape victims, which included the two women William had been found guilty of assaulting.

By this stage William had been in prison for five years. As a result of the new evidence, William was released from prison, and the charges against him were dropped. In 1985 William Jackson was awarded $720,645USD, which covered $25,000 for each year spent in prison plus lost wages and legal costs. But this in no way made up for the fact that whilst William was in prison his young son had been killed in a car accident, and he had not been allowed to attend the funeral to say goodbye.

And the implications were just as serious for Edward Jackson's other victims. In September 1982, he was found guilty of 36 charges of rape, with some of the offences going back to September 1975. This was the longest indictment in local court history at the time. Had Edward Jackson been identified as the offender earlier, some of those women would not have fallen prey to this violent, serial sexual predator.

But why was William misidentified as the offender in the first place? The two men were not doppelgangers. It was as simple as the fact that both were black males, with trimmed head hair, beards and similar physiques. However, a close evaluation of their facial features suggested only a passing resemblance. The eyewitnesses got it wrong, and race is thought to have played a significant part in this case of mistaken identity.

Dr Catriona Havard, researcher in racial bias and eyewitness identification, The Open University

And uncomfortable as this may be, race may be the crux of this whole case, from the cause of the fight that led to Snowball's death, through to what the witnesses thought they saw and who they identified, and the jury's bias in finding a young black man guilty of a violent crime for which he simply could not have been responsible.

The Crown alleged that Baker and LM acted together, attacking Snowball, and as a result of that attack he was forced backwards to his death. This sounds straightforward, but was actually a lot more ambiguous, as presented by the prosecution:

[O]ne or other or both of the accused dealt blows and/or had other contact with [S] that caused him to go through the window and that was either a punch that forced him through the window, a push that forced him through the window or as he was backing away he fell through the window. The Crown does not say that at the time either of the accused intended for him to go through the window. What we say is that was a consequence of what they did that he ended up going through the window.

Either way, the prosecution claimed that LM and Khalid were capable of being considered the legal cause of Snowball's death.

The prosecution does not need to show that the accused intended to kill the victim for a charge of murder to stand. If someone acts recklessly as to causing death or unintentionally causes death in the furtherance of certain violent crimes, or is attempting to avoid arrest, they can still be charged with murder.

However, the Crown does have to prove each of the following four elements beyond reasonable doubt for someone to be found guilty:

1. The accused committed acts that caused the victim's death
2. The accused committed said acts voluntarily
3. The accused committed these acts
   a. Intending to kill or cause serious injury, or
   b. [if reckless murder is an option for the jury to consider – as it was in this case] knowing that it was likely that death or very serious injury would result
4. The accused did not have a legal justification or excuse for the acts (for example provocation or self-defence).

So the prosecution was not alleging that either man intended to either kill Snowball or push him through the window, rather that they meant to seriously harm him. The Crown said the fight inside the party, and the altercation on the landing, showed intent by both men, Baker and LM, to cause very serious injury – there had to be *mens rea*, 'guilty mind'.

So the jury was left to decide if the Crown had established that either Baker or LM's actions caused Snowball to fall through the window to his death, and if they did, did that person mean to seriously hurt him. In essence, the jury needed to be sure that each of the above elements for murder was in place.

THE ALTERNATIVE SCENARIO

Unusually, there is not going to be a speculative alternative suspect here, as we know that the last man to touch Albert Snowball before he fell was LM. There is no doubt about this, as he has openly admitted on numerous occasions, including to police in a recorded statement that was used as inculpatory (incriminatory) evidence against him at the joint murder trial with Khalid.

The first injustice here is the fact that LM is very open about his part in what happened, the second has to be that both LM and Khalid were charged with murder.

This was a tragic accident. Neither man knew or wantonly or recklessly inflicted serious harm on Snowball. They were just trying to leave the building.

The charge of murder seems extraordinary under these circumstances – given that the Crown had no real idea how Snowball ended up going through the window. It couldn't establish if he was punched, hit, or kicked, or whether he fell backwards. No one actually saw it happen.

Regardless, 'a furious and sustained attack' was how the prosecution described the fight to the jury. The Crown painted a picture of a group of young men violently attacking partygoers at random, both inside and out on the landing of the stairwell.

But murder?

The co-accused felt the murder charge was excessive given the circumstances, too.

At one stage during the trial, LM asked if he could plead guilty to manslaughter – the Crown said yes, but on the condition that Khalid did, too. But Khalid was not about to admit to something he hadn't done, so both were stuck with fighting the murder charge.

As per their legal counsel's advice and is their right, neither Khalid or LM took the witness stand in their own defence, but the Crown, in its case against LM, did rely on his admissions made during police interview. LM said he was pushing his friend down the stairs, and the other guy (Snowball) punched him from the side, at which point LM grabbed him and pushed him backwards and he saw him stumbling backwards in reaction to the push. Then he turned away and kept walking down the stairs.

That's it, no big fight. A simple shove so he could carry on going down the stairs to get out. He said he didn't see Khalid until he got downstairs, at which point he noticed Snowball lying prone on the pavement.

THE CASE BLEW WIDE OPEN

At 18 years old, when this tragedy unfolded, Khalid Baker was one of Australia's great boxing hopes. Known as 'The Smiling Assassin', an unbeaten star athlete, he had just been chosen to represent his country at the Commonwealth Games. But of course, that all fell apart when he was charged with murder and sent to prison.

For three long years, whilst the case wound its way through the legal system and finally made it to trial, he thought he would have his day in court and then be free. His friend, LM, had always admitted being the last person to touch Albert, even though he never meant to hurt him. Snowball's death was a tragic accident.

So why would the authorities ignore that?

Even though LM and Khalid were tried simultaneously, Khalid could not use his friend's admission in his defence (known as exculpatory evidence, from the Latin meaning 'freed from blame') because the law in Victoria at the time prevented this, as the admission was made outside of a courtroom.

Remember, the two murder trials were heard concurrently by the same jury. So it must have been confusing to them when the judge, Justice Simon Whelan, said 'when you separately consider Mr Baker's case, you ignore the admissions allegedly made by [LM], they are not evidence in Mr Baker's case'.

The reason the jury was not allowed to rely on LM's admission as exculpatory evidence in the case against Khalid is that it was considered hearsay (evidence from a witness that they have not experienced personally, so they are repeating it second-hand. Hearsay evidence is generally excluded as it is not considered reliable and cannot be tested by cross-examination), and the rule (subject to some limited exceptions) at the time was that an out-of-court statement, even one made to police under caution during a recorded interview, could not be admitted as evidence of the fact asserted in that statement (i.e. in this case that LM pushed Albert). At trial the judge complied with this rule and was unsurprisingly supported in this by LM's counsel as well as the prosecutor. Baker's counsel of course fought for admission of the evidence, but to no avail.

This seems totally contradictory to the principles of natural justice, and this impenetrable and outdated law was changed soon after Khalid and LM's trial, as for a long time it had been accepted that the rule also led to the exclusion of evidence that appears perfectly reliable, as was the case here.

Sadly too late to prevent this injustice from happening.

What I also found very confusing was that the eyewitnesses provided two competing versions of events – either LM pushed the victim before he fell (as stated by LM in his admission and corroborated by Asfer and Masonga) OR Khalid did (as Doig, Arcaro, and Stuart said).

Both cannot be true, yet both men were accused of the same crime.

Realistically, only one of the men could have caused Snowball to actually fall through the window – there was no suggestion of premeditation, so we only have the Crown's assertion that they were acting in concert to seriously harm Albert. No one, not one single witness, saw both of them fighting with Snowball, so how could they be jointly responsible for his death?

It was like the prosecution was just playing the odds, not sure which case the jury would go for, so hedged its bets and prosecuted two men for the same crime, hoping that one would be found guilty.

At trial, the Crown was extremely selective with what it chose to accept from LM's recorded police interview, saying that the only element that could be relied upon was that LM had a hand in Snowball crashing through the window. The Crown rejected everything else in the statement as unreliable. The only explanation I can give is that they were cherry picking the parts of the statement they wanted to use to support their case and telling the jury to ignore the rest. Which is ridiculous, and prejudicial against Khalid.

LM did not give evidence at his trial, but his defence counsel, Mr Stuart, said his assumption that his push had caused Snowball to fall through the window was simply unfounded. He could be correct, no one knows after all. So, Stuart asked the jury to consider the three options when deciding if LM was guilty – was the fall accidental? Did LM push Snowball with the intent of causing him serious injury? Or was he the peacekeeper, trying to break up the fight?

On 25 May 2008, after a two-month trial, the jury returned a unanimous verdict for LM – not guilty of murder, or the alternatives of defensive homicide or manslaughter.

We don't know why the jurors came to their conclusion, but I can see how the jury reached their verdict, as there certainly is reasonable doubt that LM's actions intentionally led to Albert's death.

This gave Khalid great hope. He honestly believed a not guilty verdict was about to be handed down for him, too. It would defy logic for there to be any other outcome.

He waited another three days, and on 28 May he learnt his fate. Logic was defied.

Khalid Baker was found guilty of Albert Snowball's murder.

For them to have reached this conclusion, the jury must have agreed upon two things: 1) that Baker pushed Snowball, and 2) that he intended to cause him serious injury.

Khalid was stunned. And when I reviewed the case, so was I.

This despite LM's admission that he was the last person to touch the victim before he fell.

At sentencing in October 2008, Justice Whelan did acknowledge, really for the first time throughout the entire process, that although Khalid had been found guilty of murder, the moral culpability was really that of manslaughter – as there was no premeditation, no intent to kill, and no weapon used.

However, Justice Whelan added, 'Having said that, you have, by your violent acts, taken the life of an innocent young man who went to a party and became unwittingly involved in a violent confrontation which was not of his making.'

Baker was sentenced to 17 years in prison, with a non-parole period of 12 years. By this point, Khalid had already spent two years and four months of that sentence on remand waiting for the case to get to court.

In 2010, Khalid's defence submitted a petition to appeal to the Victorian Court of Appeal on the grounds that no reasonable jury could have concluded that Khalid pushed Snowball backwards with the intent of causing him a really serious injury – which is what was needed to conclude that murder was a suitable charge. In that moment, Baker had to have really wanted to hurt Albert for the charge to stand. The appeal court judges felt that the original jury had been justified in reaching the decision that they had – that Baker did intentionally seriously harm Snowball – therefore, the application for leave to appeal his conviction was refused.

In 2011, Khalid's legal team submitted a special leave to appeal to the High Court, which was granted.

One of the key grounds for the appeal was that LM's admissions were wrongly excluded in Khalid's defence at trial, and that an exception should be made to the hearsay rule in joint trials when the co-accused's admission is considered reliable – which they were considered in LM's case as they were against his penal interest (which is a statement that puts the statement maker at risk of prosecution, and by extension that the person is likely making that admission because it is true). This limited exception to the hearsay common law would bring it in line with the *Uniform Evidence Act* provisions that cover hearsay evidence when a witness is unavailable.

A further ground was that the trial judge should have directed the jury that if LM's admission was inculpatory against himself, it should be considered exculpatory in Baker's case. This is because, according to Baker's lawyers, if the Crown was going to rely on an admission as evidence of LM's guilt (which it did), it can't have it both ways and say that the same evidence doesn't speak to Baker's innocence. It is either an admission they rely on or it isn't. It's probative or it isn't.

The High Court's decision was not handed down until 15 August 2012, but the appeal judges did not feel the Crown relied upon the contents of LM's admission during police interview, and that the assertions made 'did not provide unambiguous support for the appellant's [Baker's] case'. They concluded that it was not unfair to Khalid to exclude them from his trial and that it did not occasion a miscarriage of justice in Baker's case.

They were also dismissive of LM's comment in the car, when he said in front of his friends 'Look what you made me do', as the judges felt, because Baker was driving, LM was unlikely to outright accuse him of pushing Snowball as he might be afraid that Khalid would lose control of the car as a result. They added that nothing about LM's admissions suggested that LM was taking sole responsibility for Albert's death to the exclusion of Khalid.

This ignores the fact that the other witnesses in the car said that LM said this to Faulkner, not Baker.

I find this totally confusing, as LM also didn't directly exclude anyone else either – why would he, as he knew he was the last person to touch Snowball. It would have been stranger if he had specifically stated that Baker didn't push Albert in his first interviews with police. If you've told them who did touch him, why list everyone who didn't? That would be much more suspicious, as if LM was covering for his friend.

The judges also questioned the reliability of LM's admissions – again, very strange, as even though they were damaging to LM, his own counsel did not object to their admissibility. He has at no point, since first making them to police to today, withdrawn or changed his admissions of being the last one to touch Snowball. Yet the appeal court judges decided his statements were not to be relied upon.

As a result, Baker's appeal was dismissed.

Khalid reached out to Dr Michele Ruyters, the Director of RMIT University's Bridge of Hope Innocence Initiative, to see if they could find something in the case that his lawyers had missed. After a thorough re-evaluation of the case, from the evidence from those at the house party right through to the trial and subsequent appeals, Michele could immediately see serious flaws in the prosecution.

And her conclusion? Michele believes this was a tragic accident. And she should know, as Michele and her team have spent thousands of hours reviewing all of the material available, saying, 'It's an extraordinary miscarriage of justice. There's absolutely no doubt Khalid Baker is innocent.'

The Bridge of Hope is Khalid's last chance to clear his name.

To do this, Michele submitted a petition for mercy to Victoria's Attorney General, Jill Hennessy, as although pardons are extremely rare, she does not believe that is a reason not to persevere.

EXPERT INSERT: INNOCENCE INITIATIVES

Innocence projects exist to re-examine cases where people have been found guilty, but claim to have been wrongfully convicted. Often an innocence initiative (II) will be the last port of call for people trying to clear their names, following unsuccessful appeals.

There is a long history of such projects in the US. The Innocence Project, which was founded in 1992, now claims to have worked on cases that have led to 367 exonerations, as well as 162 actual offenders being identified following the acknowledgment of a wrongful conviction and cases being reopened. Sixty-nine per cent of those exonerations have involved eyewitness misidentifications, with 42 per cent of those being cross-racial.

The aim of innocence projects is to: 1) evaluate if a miscarriage of justice has occurred, and 2) if so, discover factual or procedural evidence to support a legal avenue of exoneration. And they look at the most serious of cases – murders and sexual assaults.

No one is naïve enough these days to believe our legal system always gets it right. As a result, IIs are an invaluable element of the criminal justice system, as many people have legitimate legal defences – they may just not know their rights, or have the means to fund their own appeals. It is about bringing a fresh, unbiased perspective to cases.

Those who work in these projects have backgrounds in law, criminology, criminal justice and forensic science, and the work done often includes students undertaking work experience, with a view to training the next generation of professionals.

A core element of IIs is the fact that the practitioners understand why miscarriages of justice happen, and look for these when reviewing a case. This could be flawed expert testimony including perjured testimony (i.e. people lying about their qualifications), police or prosecutorial misconduct, poor defence representation, false testimony or confessions, or issues with eyewitness identification.

Some projects solely focus on cases where DNA is available that may exonerate an innocent person, such as Griffith University's Innocence Project in Brisbane. Not Guilty: The Sydney Exoneration Project at the University of Sydney looks at issues with memory and testimony, including false memories, false confessions, and laboratory error.

The Bridge of Hope Innocence Initiative (BOHII) is a joint venture between RMIT University in Melbourne and the Bridge of Hope Foundation, a not-for-profit organisation established in 2001 focusing on matters of social justice, the implementation of justice reinvestment, and providing emotional and physical tools to help turn disadvantaged lives around.

Specifically, the BOHII aims to look at cases where a person may have been wrongfully convicted, and assist in clearing that person's name if evidence exists to facilitate this. The BOHII investigates claims of wrongful conviction regardless of the cause or evidence available, and campaigns for reform of issues that lead to these injustices and bring about systematic changes to the criminal justice system to decrease the number of errors.

In general, the cases with which IIs are involved remain confidential – unless it is in the interest of the case to go to the media or otherwise raise public awareness.

In addition to Khalid Baker's case, which the initiative engaged with Channel Nine's *60 Minutes* to raise awareness, the BOHII also decided to work with the media to generate intelligence in the case of Keli Lane, the water polo player found guilty of murdering her two-day-old daughter, Tegan, in 1996. No body has ever been found, and Lane claims she handed the baby to her biological father at the hospital. In 2017, Lane reached out to the RMIT, as she had always maintained her innocence, but had exhausted all legal avenues of redress. The BOHII took on the case, and found several issues with the original investigation. They then worked with the ABC on a documentary about the case, entitled *Exposed: The Case of Keli Lane*, specifically to generate new information from the public – primarily trying to find either the biological father or Tegan herself. As an extension of the work with

Lane, the BOHII also submitted a petition to the Attorney General of NSW, Mark Speakman, SC MP, in December 2018, petitioning for a review of the case. At the time of writing we await to hear the outcome.

There are things that can be done to help reduce the number of people going to prison on the basis of wrongful convictions, and innocence initiatives have a significant part to play. For example, they offer a safe and controlled space for the appropriate preparation of students for a career in criminal justice fields, both educational and experiential. At an agency level, misconduct by scientific experts is highly problematic (such as Colin Manock, covered in chapter four), and amplified oversight may reduce the impact of this. Increased involvement from IIs could also help reduce wrongful convictions that result from unreliable practices by police and prosecutors, making the entire process more transparent and accountable.

We still have a long way to go, but with more innocence projects being established in Australia to tackle the problem of wrongful convictions, it is hoped that the number of people going to prison for crimes they did not commit will be reduced. And for those who do suffer miscarriages of justice, increased avenues of redress are available.

IN THE END . . .

Khalid Baker was released from prison on parole in October 2018. But the ankle monitor he wore for many months was a constant reminder of his status as a convicted murderer.

Now a 32-year-old man, Khalid Baker was 18, just a boy really, when he was found responsible for Albert Snowball's death, and had to start his new life behind bars. And HM Prison Barwon, a high risk and maximum security facility for men in Victoria, is a tough place for anyone, even a prize fighter.

For 13 years he maintained his fitness in prison, training with whatever he had to hand – using flattened toilet rolls and socks as padding – because he had never given up on his dream of winning a world title.

But the murder verdict had crushed his family, who were in court the day he was found guilty.

His sister Muna was 16 when her brother went to prison, and Urgi just eight. They lost 13 precious years with Khalid, years they can never get back. His mother, Aisha, suffered every day he was locked up. They were all terrified that something would happen to him inside, as whilst he could look after himself, he was still just eighteen.

And she was right to worry. Khalid was stabbed in the abdomen and nearly died.

The family also had to go through other traumas. Aisha was diagnosed with breast cancer, and Khalid was fearful she would die and he wouldn't be able to be there to support her. He also felt an overwhelming guilt, that he had contributed to her diagnosis due to all the stress she had been under since being charged until his release 13 years later.

The psychological trauma of injustices like this just keeps going.

But there is no doubt it is Khalid's drive, that fighting spirit, that not only makes him a champion athlete, but also keeps him fighting for justice. To clear his name.

It is that strength of mind that is spurring Khalid on.

Psychologically, he is doing better than LM, who has been racked with guilt since the night Snowball fell to his death, and his childhood friend, an innocent man, paid such a heavy price.

In December 2018 Khalid and LM had an emotional reunion – one feeling the guilt of his friend going to prison for a crime he knows he did not commit, the other feeling the injustice of 13 lost years.

LM just can't let go of the fact that if anyone should have gone to prison for what happened, it should have been him.

Another ripple of suffering that will continue.

Now Khalid is out, but he is not a free man; he still carries the title of convicted killer.

But he wants people to know the truth.

And, painful as it was, these men are bound, not only by tragedy but also love.

They also feel sadness for Snowball's family, who was only 22 years old when he died. Whilst they have both lost so much, LM and Khalid haven't forgotten the other victims of this miscarriage of justice.

So he waits to hear if the Attorney General will grant his petition for mercy and refer his case to the Court of Appeal, as this is the only way he can clear his name.

In the meantime, the Bridge of Hope Innocence Initiative also started a petition to support Khalid's right to box in matches whilst out on parole – which is currently limited as he is unable to leave Victoria, which is curtailing his ambitions to fight for Australia. At the time of writing, over 2200 people had signed this petition, myself included. (His petition can be found at change.org and is entitled 'Support Khalid Baker's request to compete in boxing matches while on parole'.)

Clearly this is also a way of raising awareness of Baker's case, and support for his petition for mercy to the Attorney General.

Meanwhile, Baker fights for redemption in the ring, too. On 11 August 2019 Khalid, ankle monitor in place, danced his way into the ring to box for the Victorian Regional Cruiserweight Title. He needed that win.

He is pure showman in the first moments as he warms up the crowd. They all know why here's here. They all know his story, and his following is growing with every match he wins.

But then it all turns serious as Khalid the fighter takes over. And wins.

In an interview after the match, Baker spoke about how special the win was, and how he is grateful for where he is today.

If this night was a metaphor for the future, Baker will soon be free from the title of murder, his conviction overturned. The man, the fighter, vindicated and free, at last. His next aim – the Australian title.

SIX

LAWYER X:
THE RISE AND FALL OF NICOLA GOBBO
(2019)

'If this gets out, say nice things at my eulogy,
because I will be gone.'

Nicola Gobbo, before it became widely known she was police informer 'Lawyer X'

It's 2008, and onlookers and diners in South Melbourne are witnesses to something they will never forget – a luxury BMW burning rapidly on a South Melbourne street. But this is no accidental car fire. This is arson. An attack on one of the city's best-known legal faces – Nicola Gobbo, defence lawyer to numerous gangland criminals.

But who would want her dead? Or was this a very public warning?

Whatever message it sent, this was certainly an explosive opener to what would later turn out to be one of the most significant events in legal history in Australia, which set a fire under Victoria's criminal justice system that would burn for years to come.

A DOUBLE-EDGED SWORD

Lawyers are proud of their right to walk both sides of the line – one day representing the Crown and the next acting in defence of the accused. But one very high profile barrister, Lawyer X, took this to unprecedented and unbelievable levels, becoming a confidential police informer whilst also representing accused criminals.

Rumours abounded, but this remained a secret for years. However, this changed in March 2019 when a suppression order was lifted, allowing Lawyer X to be identified as prominent criminal defence barrister Nicola Gobbo.

Gobbo is not the subject of a miscarriage of justice, she is the cause of many.

To put this in context, this is the biggest legal corruption case in Victoria, perhaps Australia.

It's like nothing we've ever seen before. Scandal piled on scandal.

And dangerous people may be let out of prison as a result of the fallout. This is a case of injustice on an epic scale, and the impact is going to be felt for years to come.

HOW DID IT ALL START FOR NICOLA GOBBO?

Gobbo comes from legal royalty. Her uncle, Sir James Gobbo, is a former Supreme Court judge and Governor of Victoria, and her cousin is Jeremy Gobbo QC.

Within the Melbourne legal community, Gobbo was one of the city's best known criminal barristers, but her past was chequered. In 1993, as a student living with her drug-dealing boyfriend, Brian Wilson, she was arrested for drug trafficking after a raid on their house that uncovered trafficable quantities of amphetamines and cannabis, for which she was put on a good behaviour bond with no conviction recorded.

Gobbo would get her first taste of action as a police informant the following year when the same house was raided again, and Wilson was found to still be dealing. Gobbo then turned on her former boyfriend, plotting with the police to introduce Wilson to an undercover officer.

The operation fell apart and was abandoned, partly because Gobbo was not reliable, described by Detective Senior Sergeant Jack Blayney as a loose cannon, acting in isolation and not liaising with the police.

She was admitted into legal practice in 1996, meaning she could practise law in the state of Victoria. She specialised in criminal law, and last held a certificate to practice in 2013.

She acted as an informant again in 1999. At this time, Chris Lim, a Detective Senior Constable, noted that Gobbo was very keen to become an informant, and that the police shouldn't engage with her due to her role as a lawyer.

Playing both sides was becoming a habit for Gobbo. A game almost, and one she seems to have enjoyed playing.

Nicola Gobbo did not act a formal informant again until September 2005, when she was approached by Detective Senior Constable Paul Rowe and Detective Sergeant Steve Mansell, at which time Gobbo claims Mansell told her how she could help VicPol (Victoria Police). Gobbo was a willing contributor to police intelligence gathering, and the police were very happy to have her on-board; with her legal pedigree, she was a real catch.

She remained a registered informant until at least January 2009, but was upping the stakes and the risks – by now Gobbo was also acting as defence counsel for some of Melbourne's most notorious underworld figures, including drug kingpin Tony Mokbel.

Even with the clear issues with a lawyer acting as a police source, and the many opportunities VicPol had to walk away from the situation before it blew up, they did not seek legal advice regarding conflicts of interest until 2011, and instead relied on Gobbo to 'self-regulate' her professional ethics.

By then it was far too late.

In July 2012, Neil Comrie OA APM, Chief Commissioner of Victoria Police from 1993 to 2001, was commissioned by the then Deputy Commissioner of Victoria Police, Graham Ashton AM APM, to undertake a review entitled *Victoria Police Human Source 3838 – A case review* (also known as the Comrie Review), and provided to Dannye Moloney, then Assistant Commissioner of VicPol, a confidential report relating to Gobbo's status from 2005 to 2009.

The report made a number of recommendations in terms of managing high-risk human sources and noted the dire consequences if the process is not robust. At this time, however, only a select few knew how deep the rot went.

I was fascinated with Gobbo's psychology, given she came from such a prestigious and privileged background, with the legal world as her oyster – she really could have gone all the way to become a Supreme Court judge. So why would a woman with all that power and promise risk it all to play such a dangerous game?

She certainly wasn't naïve, because she knew that she was in danger if it ever came out that she was informing on such high-profile criminals. She once said, 'If this gets out, say nice things at my eulogy, because I will be gone.'

She said that her strategy was one of plausible deniability to 'hide in plain sight'. To keep up the charade, Gobbo planned to continue her relationships with gangland criminals, and in this way convince them she was not working with the police.

It was brazen, but surely no one would suspect her?

Wrong.

Through 2006–2008 a series of 16 anonymous threats were made against her life, the content of which clearly shows that whoever the person/people were sending them, they believed she was helping police. A number of these texts were received in December 2007. Some came from public phone boxes in the form of SMS messages, and others from mobile phones registered in fictitious names.

One read: 'Hey dog we worned [sic] you not to call or talk to pigs but you being the dog call your boyfriend from Purana now you will get it dog one in the head and one in the heart.'

Another read: 'You need to get raped first them pissed on then kicked in the fucken' dog head and then shot and splattered.'

The term 'dog' is used by criminals as an insult to accuse someone of helping police.

A third simply said: 'keep your mouth shut or die.'

There were others, equally violent and threatening. In October 2007, someone left a sympathy card containing two rounds of ammunition in her letter box.

Clearly the fact that Gobbo was an informant was not a secret, and the police established Operation Gosford to investigate the threats being made against her.

The police believed an associate of the Mokbels was responsible for the threats. But they also knew that the list of those who could pose a threat to Lawyer X was very extensive – including not only those Gobbo had directly acted for, but also their family, associates and friends, or any other people employed by affected criminal organisations seeking payback.

But she didn't stop, remaining a registered source until early 2009, and even after that she kept passing information to Victoria Police until 2010.

And threats weren't just made against Gobbo herself. In 2014 an anonymous threatening letter was sent to her eldest child.

By 2014, Lawyer X's identity was one of the worst kept secrets in town.

But the compromise of her identity had started much earlier. On 15 November 2005, VicPol undertook a risk assessment in relation to Informant 3838, which detailed the risks to the 'source' (as informants are known) of compromise. It stated that the source was acting for a number of members of the Mokbel criminal cartel, including kingpin Tony. It goes on to note that the group considered 'breaches of their criminal code of silence as a matter of extreme concern' and was known to employ extreme violence – meaning Gobbo was in danger.

In this same risk assessment, her handler noted a number of potential sources of compromise, any one of which could put her safety at risk. These included the fact her handlers believed Gobbo had had intimate relationships with some police officers, and specifically that she appears to 'enjoy the company of male Police members', and is friends with others. The fact that she had also been in professional contact with police from various task forces as well as the fact that the Major Drug Investigation Division (MDID) knew Gobbo was a police informant was also noted as a concern, even more so as the handler believed it highly likely unidentified close colleagues of those police also knew.

Gobbo herself stated that 'the whole world knows who Lawyer X is now'.

In a letter to police in 2015, Gobbo asserted her motivation in assisting police was not for self-gain (as she claims not to have been paid for any of the information she passed on), but was 'borne from the frustration of being aware of prolific large commercial drug trafficking, importations of massive quantities of drugs, murders, bashings, perverting the course of justice, huge money laundering and other serious offences all being committed without any serious inroads being made by Police'. (The whole letter can be read online.)

Balance this declaration against the fact that Gobbo's current partner, and possibly the father of her two children, Richard Barkho, is currently serving a minimum of five years in prison on drug charges . . .

She also said she was upset at the criminals' ability to use lawyers to manipulate situations for personal benefit. At other times Gobbo has claimed her sole reason for turning informer was to escape the clutches of the Mokbel cartel.

Clearly, there was a mix of motivations for Gobbo to act as an informer. But equally as obvious was that she seemed to enjoy playing the agent provocateur – a dangerous game of cat and mouse she'd begun way back in 1995.

THE CASE THAT BROUGHT HER UNSTUCK

It all started to unravel for Gobbo in 2008, when she was called as a witness in the most significant police corruption case in Victoria's history.

Gobbo had been asked to wear a wire to record a conversation with former drug detective Paul Dale, who had been charged with the burglary of a drug house in 2003 (a charge of which he was never convicted). Dale had gone up against Gobbo many times in court, as she defended accused drug traffickers, and he had suggested to people he arrested that they contact Gobbo to represent them.

So it was natural to him that as soon as he was charged over the burglary, he contacted Gobbo himself. When Dale told Gobbo about the charges, he claims she agreed to act for him pro bono. She denies ever formally being retained as his lawyer.

Regardless, the plot thickened as in 2008 detectives from Victoria Police believed Dale was involved with the execution-style murder of Terrence Hodson and his wife, Christine, who were shot dead in their home in 2004. Taskforce Petra was established to investigate these murders, and the allegation was that Dale had wanted Mr Hodson dead as he was due to testify against Dale in court relating to the theft of drugs and cash from his property. The two had been known to each other, as Hodson was a police informant and Dale was his handler.

Another thread in this tangled web: police alleged that Dale organised for Mr Hodson to be assassinated by underworld murderer and drug dealer Carl Williams – another of Gobbo's clients. Williams had stated that he had been asked by Dale to organise the hit on Hodson and had paid for the murder.

The evidence the police used in their case against Williams came from a conversation Gobbo captured with Dale during covert surveillance. Gobbo had gone further, giving legal paperwork Dale had allegedly supplied her with after he was charged with drug offences straight to her handlers at VicPol. She was literally working with the police to see her clients successfully prosecuted.

Initially Gobbo said she would be willing to give evidence against Dale (who at that stage had also been charged with Hodson's murder and who spent some eight months in remand awaiting trial before the case against him was dropped). The steering committee into the murders – which included Police Commissioner Graham Ashton and Deputy Commissioner Simon Overland – ignored the warnings that this could put Gobbo in very significant danger.

The risks kept ramping up for Gobbo, and in 2010 VicPol was very worried for her safety if she was called as a prosecution witness in their case against Dale, as it would identify her as a police informant. They applied for a suppression order, to keep her identity a secret, but it was refused. In April, media outlets published Gobbo's name and stated she was to be called as a witness in the committal hearing against Dale.

She refused to give evidence at that trial, and later sued Victoria Police, saying they had not only ruined her career, but had put her life in serious danger. (The details of the payout are subject to a confidentiality agreement as it was settled out of court.)

And as it turned out, her life had been put in danger for nothing, because the charges against Dale (who has consistently denied any wrongdoing) were later dropped for lack of evidence.

Being listed as a witness in the murder trial had really put her on the map, in all the wrong ways, and legal colleagues advised her she was becoming too close to her clients.

Little did they know.

Regardless of the obvious risks, some police handlers were still really keen to take advantage of the information Lawyer X could provide, as well as assistance with tactical advice about the disruption of individuals' and organised crime groups' activities.

But by now, the problems of Lawyer X's duplicity were becoming far too clear to everyone. After media revelations that VicPol used a confidential informant they named as Lawyer X, the Chief Commissioner of Victoria Police made a notification to the Victorian Independent Broad-based Anti-corruption Commission (IBAC), which initiated an inquiry into the situation.

The IBAC appointed Murray Kellam QC, a retired judge, to investigate what had been happening. This inquiry's report was called the *Report Concerning Victoria Police Handling of Human Source Code Name 3838* (also called the Kellam Report). Kellam handed down his findings in February 2015, although a redacted version wasn't made publicly available until April 2019.

The implications were obvious, and in the Kellam Report the author noted that Gobbo's informing to police had the potential to 'undermine the convictions of a number of people', listing seven that were possibly contaminated, and that it represented police negligence 'of the highest order'. And these were seven very dangerous people.

A recommendation was that a copy of the report be made available to the Director of Public Prosecutions (DPP), John Champion SC, by the Chief Commissioner of Victoria Police, Graham Ashton (which was duly done), and that the DPP should consider whether any prosecutions based on information provided by VicPol had resulted in a miscarriage of justice as a result of the conduct of a barrister acting for them.

The DPP in each State and Territory (and at the Commonwealth level) is, of course, bound by the duty of disclosure (although, as we have seen, they don't always comply with this obligation, such as Andrew Mallard's case in chapter three and Henry Keogh's in chapter four), which 'obliges the prosecution to make available to an accused person all material upon which the prosecution intends to rely and any credible material that may be helpful to the accused's case. This duty is an integral part of the prosecution's role in ensuring a fair trial and continues after the conclusion of court proceedings'.

And the danger of miscarriages of justice happening was very real. In 2016 Champion produced his own report: The *Report of the Director of Public Prosecutions in Relation to Recommendation 12 of the Kellam Report*, or the Champion Report, which outlined that between September 2005 and January 2009, Lawyer X appeared in 304 separate hearings, on behalf of 143 different people, in matters prosecuted by the DPP.

It was all too messy to keep quiet now.

The DPP recognised and acted on his legal obligation as a prosecutor to disclose the relevant information from the IBAC report to anyone who may have been adversely affected by Gobbo's breaches of client privilege whilst informing to VicPol. This of course included Gobbo's clients who had been found guilty of serious criminal offences, with the DPP focusing specifically on seven individuals, all of whom were members of the Mokbel cartel (a nickname established by Gobbo's counsel when referring to those involved with drug manufacture and trafficking as part of Tony Mokbel's criminal empire in Melbourne).

Tony Mokbel himself as the drug kingpin is serving at least

22 years in prison. Zlate Cvetanovski (a Mokbel associate arrested in 2006 over his involvement in a Mokbel-controlled drug lab) has just been released on bail and, at the time of writing, is appealing all three of his convictions. Four others, Milad Mokbel (Tony's brother), George Peters, Frank Ahec, and Kamel (Karl) Khoder have all completed their prison sentences, and Darren Bednarski received a suspended sentence.

In addition to telling these seven men that Gobbo was an informant, the DPP also wanted to inform them that she had provided information to VicPol about other persons for whom she acted as legal counsel, who then made statements against a number of the affected persons. The water was getting murkier and murkier.

This was a huge call for the DPP, but what choice did he have? It was legally and ethically indefensible not to release the information, given that clear breaches of legal process had taken place that would be impossible to keep quiet.

The Director wrote a letter to the Chief Commissioner of Victoria Police in 2016, which provided a copy of the disclosure he planned to make to Mokbel and his six associates. It read:

> IBAC produced a confidential report (the 'Kellam Report') last year, relating to the use by Victoria Police of a certain legal practitioner (to whom I will refer as '3838') as a registered human source – that is, a police informer.
>
> The matter that I wish to disclose to you is that the material contained in the Kellam Report could be interpreted to mean that at or about a time when 3838 was your legal representative in relation to charges for which you were later convicted, 3838 was also providing information to Victoria Police about you, in possible breach of legal professional privilege and/or in breach of a duty of confidentiality.

The DPP added another paragraph to the disclosure letters to Tony and Milad Mokbel, as well as Ahec and Cvetanovski, stating that:

> Further, I wish to disclose to you that some material contained in the Kellam Report could also be interpreted to mean that certain persons who made statements against you, in the matters for which you were convicted, may have been legally represented by 3838 at or about the same time that 3838 was providing information to Victoria Police about those persons, and possible breach of legal professional privilege and/or in breach of a duty of confidentiality.

This was clearly explosive. This decision by the DPP would rock the legal and criminal justice world in Victoria to its foundation.

By this point the physical danger to Lawyer X had become severe.

On 23 March 2016, the Deputy Commissioner (Special Operations) of VicPol, Shane Patton, informed the DPP that, following a further risk assessment, the planned disclosures would 'increase the likelihood of EF's [Gobbo's] death from "possible" to "almost certain" and the overall risk of death from "high" to "extreme"'.

Lawyer X clearly knew the danger, too, as she contended that once the DPP sent the disclosure letters to the seven persons listed, including the Mokbel brothers, that the contents would become generally known and would be leaked to the media, and the details published. Gobbo believed she would then be killed, either by one of the seven or another criminal for whom she had acted as counsel.

At this stage the Chief Commissioner of Victoria Police and Gobbo initiated separate proceedings in the Supreme Court to prevent the DPP from releasing the information, as although the

letters did not name the informer directly (instead calling her informant 3838), they claimed that it would put Gobbo and her two
children in extreme mortal danger, and potentially dissuade other
informants from providing confidential assistance to police in
the future

They were right; any disclosure that 3838 was their legal representative would have made it completely obvious who they were
talking about. The DPP accepted this, but stated that Gobbo was
aware that there was no absolute protection as an informant under
the law.

She had even stood in court and been told that whilst representing Tony Mokbel as junior counsel in 2005 in a subpoena
application, when they were seeking information from the Office
of Police Integrity on just this issue – informers and police officers
who had investigated drug-related criminal offences.

In that case Justice William Gillard, confirmed that an exception
to an informer's right to protection already existed 'where on the trial
of a defendant for a criminal offence, disclosure of the identity of the
informer could help to show that the defendant was innocent of
the offence. In that case, and in that case only, the balance falls on the
side of disclosure'.

Oh the irony, that Gobbo was in court representing Mokbel and
to have heard that her own identity as a confidential source might
one day be released given the right legal circumstances.

A five-year legal battle ensued to keep Gobbo's name a secret,
which ended up in the Supreme Court. The hearings were held in
closed court, and those affected (i.e. Gobbo's ex-clients) were not
informed and publications of the proceedings were suppressed.

In June 2017, the Supreme Court made its decision. Justice
Timothy Ginnane, who oversaw the process, acknowledged that
police informants are an important element of the criminal justice

system, and that they and their families need protection. However, he felt that the overwhelming public interest in the right to a fair trial with the assistance of independent legal counsel outweighed this.

I have to agree with this position – regardless of who the defendant is, and what we may think of their general criminality, they have a right to be considered innocent until proven guilty fairly.

The decision was appealed, but the Court of Appeal dismissed the case as the court considered the public interest outweighed the possible dangers, and in that case disclosures were not protected by public interest immunity, which would normally prevent the identification of police informants. The court also noted that the State (including the police as officers for the State) must be, and be seen to be, fair in the administration of justice, including all processes involved, to maintain public confidence in due process.

But VicPol and Gobbo were given leave to appeal to the High Court, which they did. Again they failed, as in November 2018 the High Court revoked permission to seek further appeals. But they ordered the outcome would be suppressed until December 2018, and an interim order preventing the wider release of Lawyer X's true identity was established until 1 March 2019.

VicPol and Gobbo had now exhausted all legal avenues to keep her identity a secret, as all three courts had agreed that the public interest in disclosure to those affected outweighed the public interest in protecting the source's identity.

This legal process of reporting, hearings and appeals had taken several years, and cost Victoria Police millions of dollars.

And all of this happened in secret – all subject to suppression orders until the process was complete.

On 1 March 2019, the newly established Royal Commission identified Gobbo on its website as it was really beginning to ramp up its investigation.

In a bold move, the Commission also publicised Gobbo's photograph in Victorian prisons, as well as in *The Age* and *Herald Sun* newspapers. The purpose of disseminating her identity in this way was that the Commission was seeking submissions from people who had either been represented by Lawyer X, or who otherwise felt their conviction may have been affected due to her dual role as legal counsel and confidential police informant.

The seriousness of the problem was finally laid bare, before the public, when the court noted in its summation that the prosecutorial procedures and outcomes had been 'corrupted in a manner which debased fundamental premises of the criminal justice system'. They went on to add that Gobbo's activities represented 'fundamental and appalling' breaches of her duties, to both the courts and her clients, and damningly that 'Victoria Police were guilty of reprehensible conduct in knowingly encouraging [Ms Gobbo] to do as she did and were involved in sanctioning atrocious breaches of the sworn duty of every police officer to discharge all duties imposed on them faithfully and accordingly to law without favour or affection, malice or ill-will'.

HOW WE GOT HERE: MELBOURNE'S GANGLAND KILLINGS AND GOBBO'S RISE TO INFAMY

From mid-2003 to July 2004, Gobbo met Detective Sergeant Stuart Bateson of the Purana Taskforce, Victoria's anti-gangland task force established after a number of underworld murders and to fight the growing problem of gangland crime in Melbourne, as at the time there was a drug war playing out between various syndicates.

This had all started in 1998 with the murder of Alphonse Gangitano, an underworld figure and face of Melbourne's Carlton Crew, a criminal organisation that had been established in Melbourne in the 1970s.

The violence quickly ramped up, particularly after infamous underground figure Carl Williams (a convicted murderer and drug trafficker, as well as an associate of the Mokbels), was shot in the stomach by brothers Mark and Jason Moran because he owed the family $80,000. Williams survived, but this event initiated a long line of murders, which became known as the 'Melbourne gangland murders'.

Mark Moran was shot and killed in June 2000, and his brother Jason was murdered alongside Pasquale Barbaro whilst sitting in a minivan in front of 10 small children in 2003. This shocking double murder, which happened at the end of a children's football clinic so there were lots of innocent adults and children who saw the shootings, was an escalation in violence. As a result, Purana was given significant increased resources.

Members of the task force were now under a lot of pressure from those above to put an end to the gang warfare, prevent further shootings and stop the flow of methamphetamine through Melbourne.

The police believed that a number of the shootings and murders were being carried out by hit men from the various criminal organisations in Melbourne (which later became immortalised in popular culture through the 2008 TV series *Underbelly*). They were keen to clean up the streets to stop the killings.

The police were being hampered in their efforts to fight the gangland criminals, as no one was talking. So informants were essential if they wanted to dismantle the criminal networks that were taking over the streets from the inside out.

Taskforce Purana was divided into two phases; the first focused on Carl Williams and the murders that occurred after he was shot, and the second looked largely at Tony Mokbel's criminal activity.

Gobbo was a godsend to both phases of Purana, as she was heavily involved with both Williams and Mokbel. She began passing information to the task force, on the understanding it would be treated with the strictest confidence. One of the snippets she passed on was information about a barrister and solicitor who was acting as a messenger between Williams whilst he was in prison and associates on the outside, including Tony Mokbel.

The police must have been ecstatic, having someone like Gobbo in their corner. They needed an edge, as between 16 January 1998 and 13 August 2010, 36 Melbourne criminals were murdered. Blood was running through the streets, and the result was that there was a huge power vacuum in the Melbourne criminal underworld, as the Calabrian Mafia-linked 'Carlton Crew' and the Carl Williams gang fought for supremacy and control of the drug trade.

But Gobbo wasn't the only one playing both sides. By 2004, pressure was mounting on Tony Mokbel's cartel, which was aligned with Carl Williams, as the gangland wars and subsequent murders were getting out of control. So Mokbel arranged to meet with Detective Sergeant Martin Robertson and a colleague (who cannot be named). This conversation was secretly recorded and a transcript made available to the Royal Commission in 2019.

During this chat, Mokbel proposed a radical plan that he said would bring peace to the streets, and would ease the pressure on the police and court system. The police desperately wanted information on the gangland murders that had been plaguing Melbourne, which the meeting suggests Mokbel was actually trying to stop, to the extent that he said that he and three of his associates would be willing to 'do a little bit of time' if it would end the drug war by 'leaving the streets' to the police for a while.

This meeting came within weeks of the death of Andrew Veniamin, once described as one of Australia's busiest hit men, who predominantly worked for Carl Williams. The murder was discussed, as was the killing of drug dealer Michael Marshall and

Jason Moran (who had been shot in the car with Pasquale Barbaro in 2003).

But Mokbel also wanted to broker a deal with then Director of Public Prosecutions, Paul Coghlan, that would limit any charges against him relating to drug offences. That deal never came off, partly because Head of the Purana Taskforce, Jim O'Brien, thought that Mokbel was arrogant in thinking his plan could end the bloodshed.

Mokbel was later charged and found guilty of multiple drug offences, for which he is currently serving at least 22 years in prison, although he was acquitted of the murder of Jason Moran and the charges against him in relation to Marshall's murder were dropped.

Most of the murders remain unsolved to this day, but officers from Purana think Carl Williams was responsible for 10 of them, as he in essence started a war with the Morans after they shot him. He wanted to get rid of the entire family and their associates. Williams pleaded guilty to three murders in 2007 and the conspiracy to murder a fourth person, and in exchange for the plea the police withdrew two other murder charges. He was sentenced to life with a minimum of 35 years non-parole.

We will never see justice for any other murders he may be responsible for, as Williams died in Barwon Prison (a maximum security prison in Victoria) in 2010, after he was attacked by another inmate with the stem of an exercise bike the day after a front-page *Herald Sun* story ran about him.

He was the last murder victim of Melbourne's notorious gangland killings.

When the world found out that Gobbo had operated as a police informant whilst also acting as a defence lawyer, doubt was placed on the reliability of any conviction she was ever involved with. And as we have seen, she was working for some of Melbourne's most serious and violent criminals.

Gobbo was certainly prolific, claiming she provided information to police that has contributed to 386 arrests and convictions, and there are 5500 information reports in the police system associated with her.

Inevitably, the truth finally came out. Anthony Dowsley and Patrick Carlyon, both reporters for the *Herald Sun*, broke the case, for which they were jointly awarded the Gold Quill, amongst other awards, from the Melbourne Press Club in 2018. But they kept their secret until the Court of Appeal suppression order was lifted, after it was ruled that the integrity of the criminal justice system trumped the need to keep one woman's identity a secret.

The fallout was just starting.

THE LAWYER X COMMISSION

The Royal Commission into the Management of Police Informants opened on 15 February 2019, with hearings being held at the Fair Work Commission in Melbourne.

The Commission has legal teeth – it can compel people to give evidence, for example, but it can't change or overturn sentences, release people from custody, or order retrials. However, the results can certainly be used by those affected to challenge the legality of their convictions, a situation that has already come to fruition.

The opening statement notes that 'This Commission results from the conduct of a former legal practitioner and her relationship with Victoria Police' and that the authorised expenses to undertake the inquiry were capped at $7.5 million. That's a huge amount of taxpayers' money to be spent, but then corruption on this scale is largely unheard of; and it was going to get a lot more expensive yet. That's on top of what has already been spent by VicPol to try to keep Gobbo's identity a secret. It's extraordinary.

But then nothing about this case is ordinary.

The Commission needed to determine how many, and to what extent, criminal cases have been adversely affected by Gobbo playing for both sides simultaneously. The Commission also had a responsibility to look at VicPol's management of privileged sources, the use of information obtained from informers, and recommend measures to address any failures.

There were two deadlines set. Everything relating to Gobbo specifically and what cases may have been tainted through her involvement had to be reported on by 1 July 2019, as this was seen as the most time critical as the Commission was aware that people may have had legal recourse if miscarriages of justice had occurred. The remaining elements had to be reported on by 1 December 2019.

Initially, the Commission's remit was limited to VicPol's use of Gobbo as a privileged police informant across a five-year period from 2005 to 2009. However, once the Commission started gathering information, it became clear that her connections to the police went back much further. The scope of the inquiry was therefore extended to cover the entire period Gobbo had been a source, 1993–2009, over 17 years.

As a result of the lengthy period and increased size and complexity of the investigation, the Victorian Government extended the reporting period to July 2020. Costs also rocketed, and the government provided an extra $20.5 million dollars to the inquiry.

The situation the Commission faces is unique, and there are no legal procedures or precedents for them to rely on in order to determine how to proceed.

The Commission had a number of points to investigate and report on under their terms of reference, perhaps most notably:

1. The number of, and extent to which, cases may have been affected by the conduct of EF as a human source.

   . . .

4. The current use of human source information in the criminal justice system from human sources who are subject to legal obligations of confidentiality or privilege.

(All of the documents from the Royal Commission are available from https://www.rcmpi.vic.gov.au/hearings.)

Even the Commission process itself has been slightly farcical, with Commissioner Margaret McMurdo AC dubbing the process 'a magical mystery tour', with progress frustrated by delayed and fragmentary information being provided to the Commission by VicPol, and no one seems to know where it will end.

It was essential to keep going, however, as exemplified by McMurdo when she said, 'when those whom the community entrusts to uphold and enforce the law themselves breach fundamental legal obligations, confidence in our justice system, and indeed our democracy, is seriously diminished'. Very true.

As of July 2019, when an interim report was published, the Commission had heard from 32 witnesses over 22 days of hearings, and had issued 374 Notices to Produce (a notice that legally compels someone to provide documents) and requests for information, which resulted in the production of more than 58,000 documents.

One of the witnesses called to give evidence was Paul Dale. He had spent years waiting for the opportunity to share his side of the story, and the Royal Commission gave him his chance.

He was so emotional whilst giving his testimony that at times his voice shook. He stated that his conversation with Gobbo was subject to client privilege, and that using Gobbo as a source and the recording against him at trial was a perversion of justice. It is hard to argue against this.

Another bombshell came out as part of the process – police suspected that whilst Gobbo was informing to them, she was also informing *on* them, to her underworld associates.

Evidence for this comes from Stuart Bateson, who was part of the Purana Taskforce from October 2003 to 2007. Bateson made a statement at the request of the Royal Commission, in which he details his contact with Gobbo. At various times he was in charge of the task force, and received information the nature of which led him to believe it had been provided by Lawyer X. He knew her real identity, but always kept it confidential. In his redacted statement, however, he also made several references to calls made to him by Gobbo, in which he got the sense she was 'fishing for information from me' in regards to comments she was making about her clients, and that he 'did not recall engaging with her on the topic'.

Remember, she only had access to the task force because she was an informant, but was using that to leverage information from them to help those she was representing as a criminal defence lawyer.

She really wanted it all ways round.

And the police weren't exactly trusting of her as a result. A statement by Paul Rowe, also produced as part of the 2019 Royal Commission, states that he met Gobbo in 2005, when he was a Detective Senior Constable at the MDID, which at the time was investigating drug manufacture by the Mokbel cartel.

When Darren Bednarski was arrested by members of the MDID, Rowe carried out the formal police interview. Bednarski asked to speak to Gobbo, and Rowe called her. Rowe had never met Gobbo before, but he was aware that she and other lawyers were suspected of having personal relationships with Tony Mokbel and had 'reputations for providing protection for him through their role as lawyers. My view was that Ms Gobbo and others would assist him to influence the criminal justice process and in turn help him to avoid prosecution'. Rowe suspected that Gobbo assisted Tony Mokbel by trying to ensure that when his associates were arrested they did not implicate him, and that she sought information for Mokbel and fed it directly back to him.

And the Commission is still on a fact-finding mission – hoping that now Gobbo's identity has been released, more people who fear their cases may have been tainted by her breach of client privilege will come forward and provide information.

December 2019 was a roller coaster at the Royal Commission, with many high-ranking current and ex-members of Victoria Police giving evidence.

One of which was Simon Overland, ex-Chief Commissioner of Victoria Police, who had a focus on Melbourne's gang wars. Overland told the Commission that Nicola Gobbo was already in trouble, even before she was recruited as a confidential informant, saying that she 'had become a facilitator of criminal conduct, not a legal adviser'.

Gobbo herself was called, but tried to avoid giving evidence by claiming she was psychologically unfit – that she lives in fear and is suicidal, and if forced to take the stand may have a 'psychotic mental health breakdown' as she has been diagnosed with a major depressive disorder as well as post-traumatic distress.

Her pleas to be excused were rejected.

When Gobbo gave evidence in February 2020 she did so over the phone, after her lawyers won the battle to keep her location a secret. She also wanted to keep her face out of court, even though everyone by now knew full well what she looks like – or we did, as there is some suggestion she has changed her appearance, no doubt to protect her life.

When she spoke it became clear that both she and her police handlers knew full well that her actions were well beyond unethical, and could in fact be perverting the course of justice.

After the Commission closed submissions in April 2019, Victoria's Director of Public Prosecutions, Kerri Judd QC, needed to navigate a minefield and decide how many cases would need to be retired, or even offenders released. Further, those found guilty on the basis of Gobbo's information may have the right to compensation.

THE IMPLICATIONS FOR VICTORIA POLICE ARE STAGGERING

At least some within the VicPol ranks totally disregarded the law when using Gobbo to inform on her clients, as well as asking a practising attorney to wear a wire to ensnare their own officers in crime.

There is no doubt now this has, and will continue, to result in miscarriages of justice.

But it has to be done.

By the time the Commission sat in February 2019, three people were already appealing their convictions on the basis that Gobbo affected their prosecutions and trial. By July 2019 it had been acknowledged that 40 cases may be revisited as a result of being caught up in the Lawyer X scandal.

And the first example has already hit the courts, which focused on the conviction of Faruk Orman, who was in prison for the murder of underworld figure Victor Peirce in 2002. Orman was jailed in 2009, sentenced to 20 years with a minimum of 14 years, after acting as a getaway driver.

In February 2019 he filed a petition of mercy with the Attorney General, and amongst other points, his submission alleged he was denied a fair trial as a result of Gobbo's conduct and her role as an informant for VicPol.

The query here had nothing to do with Mokbel and his crew, but rather rested with the fact that in October 2002 Gobbo was counsel for 'Witness Q', who was a key prosecution witness in a murder case against Orman, as Witness Q was the only person that could put Orman at the scene of Victor Peirce's murder in Port Melbourne when he was gunned down in his car. According to

Witness Q, Orman had confessed to being the getaway driver for the hitman, Andrew Veniamin.

Oddly, in October 2006 Gobbo also became Orman's lawyer, to represent him against the murder charges he was facing. But in November 2007, whilst still acting for Orman (who has always maintained his innocence), Gobbo called her contact in VicPol and told them their case against Orman was about to disintegrate, as she knew Witness Q was having second thoughts about testifying, so she suggested they pay Witness Q a visit to ensure he testified.

How did Gobbo know? Well, Witness Q was still a client of hers. In that way Gobbo helped to ensure that Witness Q gave evidence against Orman at the murder trial, who was subsequently found guilty and sentenced to 20 years in prison.

This was a bizarre situation.

In July 2019, at the Supreme Court of Victoria, the Crown conceded that, as a result of Gobbo's call to police in November 2007, there was 'a substantial miscarriage of justice'. This happened simultaneous to the Commission investigating Victoria Police's use of informants.

Orman, then 37, was subsequently acquitted of murder and walked free from a Melbourne court after spending 12 years in prison – the first man to have his conviction overturned as a result of the Lawyer X scandal.

Prosecutors agreed that whilst Witness Q's statement was still available should prosecutors wish to use it, it would be 'unjust' to seek a retrial under these circumstances.

There are multiple miscarriages of justice here. Firstly, Gobbo breached her client privilege, which meant Orman did not get a fair trial. Secondly, where is the justice in this for the murder victim, Victor Peirce, whose murderer (whoever that be) is still unknown? All because Victoria Police used a lawyer to act as an informant.

Orman's release puts heaps more pressure on Victoria Police, above and beyond the impact of the Commission.

And there are more to come.

Tony Mokbel received a 30-year sentence, with a minimum of 22 years without parole, for drug trafficking, including 12 years for smuggling cocaine. Gobbo represented Mokbel seven times between 2002 and 2006, and specifically as junior counsel in 2005, a few days after she registered as a police informant. Whilst acting as his legal counsel, she was informing VicPol on his plans to fight extradition charges as well as how to restrict his movements around Melbourne. Given that Mokbel thought he was receiving independent legal advice, he now has grounds to appeal as he can argue he did not receive a fair trial.

Regardless of what you think of Mokbel, he does have a point. All because Gobbo wanted to be out from under Mokbel, and would have done anything to get him arrested. At least that's what she claims.

Mokbel is now challenging his conviction, in the wake of the Lawyer X scandal, and you can see how he could have a good shot at claiming a miscarriage of justice has occurred.

That is if he survives prison. On 10 February 2019 the *Herald Sun* ran a news article about Mokbel and his life behind bars, saying 'Gangland drug lord Tony Mokbel has transformed from street boss to powerful enforcer at Barwon Prison, with fears he could be continuing to call the shots beyond the prison walls'. The article went on to say that he was disrupting an extortion racket being run by Pacific Islander inmates. This clearly angered fellow inmates, to the point that the day after the article ran, Mokbel (then 53) was stabbed multiple times with a jail-made shiv by two Pacific Islander inmates. He was injured so badly he was placed in an induced coma. He has now recovered, but required ongoing protection for months.

This is famously not the first time we have seen an inmate attacked after a news story ran; Carl Williams was murdered the day after the *Herald Sun* ran a piece on him. Perhaps Mokbel will now keep his head down, at least until he hears if he has been granted an appeal.

One of the other primary people Gobbo's testimony affected was George Peters, the drug cartel's 'cook'. On 23 February 2002, Peters was arrested and charged in relation to the manufacture of methamphetamine. He was arrested again on similar charges in April 2003, and remained in custody until December when he was bailed.

Gobbo acted for Peters between 2002 and 2006, both before and during the time she was an informant. She represented Peters at hearings in relation to both the 2002 and 2003 drugs charges.

Between October 2005 and April 2006, Gobbo gave her VicPol handlers information about crimes Peters had been involved with other than those he was involved with in 2002 and 2003, and for which he had previously been charged. This information led to evidence being obtained that led to Peters' arrest in 2006 on additional charges.

Gobbo has described Peters as a compulsive gambler and heavy drug user, but also as another victim of the Mokbels – alleging he was pressured into making the drugs, sometimes at gunpoint.

As soon as Peters was arrested in 2006 he called Gobbo. She spoke to her client both before and after his formal police interview, and Peters made admissions to police.

On 8 February 2007, Peters pleaded guilty to numerous charges in relation to drugs manufacture and possessing an unregistered handgun, and was sentenced to 10 years in prison, with a minimum of seven years before parole.

Then there's Tony Mokbel's brother, Milad, also involved in the family drug trafficking business. Gobbo knew Peters very well.

She was his friend (she once even babysat his children), and told the police that if they wanted to get Milad, they needed to roll the cook. She also told police that, if they could get Peters to talk, he knew enough about Milad to put him away for a long time.

She was setting Peters up to become an informant.

During her time with Peters, he had shared information about a couple of houses where he 'cooked' the drugs, and in 2006 this included details of when and where Peters was dropping drugs off to Milad Mokbel. Police swooped, and in April 2006 arrested the cook, Milad Mokbel and Zlate Cvetanovski.

The cook talked, as Gobbo had given the police the information they needed to break him, and he was desperate to minimise the penalty he would receive.

Peters ended up helping the police, and delivered drugs to targets, including Milad Mokbel, after which the cook was re-arrested. He kept assisting VicPol though, and made many statements that were used in subsequent prosecutions.

Gobbo later contended that she did not influence Peters to plead guilty, however it is clear that both VicPol and Lawyer X were actively targeting the Mokbels' associates to dismantle the network, and that included Peters.

The Director of Public Prosecutions would argue that Peters had a right to know that Gobbo was an informer under disclosure rules, especially as he was specifically used to get information on Milad Mokbel, and that his decision to plead guilty would have been influenced by the legal advice Gobbo gave him, which was potentially not in his best interests but rather hers and VicPol's. In that way, a miscarriage of justice on procedural grounds could be argued to have occurred and that his conviction should be quashed.

Guess who Milad Mokbel called when he was arrested as part of the sting? Lawyer X. Gobbo did not formally act for him, as she was already retained by Peters. Instead Gobbo helped the police by arranging for the recording of a telephone intercept to capture information that would incriminate Milad Mokbel.

Milad Mokbel was also charged and found guilty, and in 2008 received 11 years and eight months for trafficking methamphetamine and dealing with the proceeds of crime. Further, Milad Mokbel was charged with additional drug crimes and blackmail, and in 2011 was sentenced to four years' in jail.

Milad Mokbel pleaded guilty to the charges, but that does not mean his conviction is without legal issue – the Supreme Court judge believes that Milad Mokbel had a right to know how the information used to catch him was procured, that Gobbo was the informant, and that the provided legal advice to his co-accused made Mokbel's conviction unsafe, as it involved an abuse of process because it relied on Peters' evidence.

Another of the seven associated with Tony Mokbel and his drug empire who was named by the DPP as someone who should be informed about Gobbo's activities as an informant was Kamel Khoder, who was the money man for the Mokbels, providing false tax records and employment histories, as well as fraudulent home loans. Lawyer X's handlers were particularly interested in getting information on Khoder because the Purana Taskforce was focused on methodically removing from play Tony Mokbel's associates, all to destabilise his activities.

In 2006 Khoder was charged with 15 counts of making a false document, and 18 counts of obtaining a financial advantage by deception. In August 2007 Khoder met Gobbo to discuss the charges against him. They had numerous conversations about the charges, and Khoder told Gobbo he intended to defend them. Gobbo then passed that information to her handlers. This helped VicPol undermine his defence. In one example, Lawyer X told them that Khoder planned to arrange for a building in Sydney to be burnt down to destroy documents that would incriminate him. He later decided to plead guilty, and the police told Gobbo that this was as a result of her advice.

Gobbo then went on to arrange a plea deal for him, negotiating the charges on which he would plead guilty. At his plea hearing he agreed to give evidence against others, and provided a witness statement to that affect in court.

Khoder was subsequently convicted of money laundering, and received a sentence of two years and two months, which was wholly suspended.

Khoder could argue that his conviction is unsafe because Gobbo was intentionally seeking information that would assist in his prosecution, and that she persuaded him to plead guilty to further her own and VicPol's causes. By providing information to police about his defence whilst acting for him, she clearly breached her professional duties, and it could be contended this represents yet another miscarriage of justice.

There are others, many others. Gobbo stated in her letter to police in 2015 that there were 386 people that she was specifically aware of, that were either arrested or charged as a result of the information she provided to police. However, there were probably more that she was not aware of, as her information was of such significant value.

In April 2019, Cvetanovski appealed to have his conviction overturned on the basis of Gobbo's involvement in his prosecution. Victoria's Court of Appeal granted his leave to appeal in May 2020, and he was given bail and released from prison.

With the exception of Cvetanovski, the others all pleaded guilty to the charges against them. Under normal circumstances, a conviction based on a guilty plea cannot be overturned.

But these are not normal circumstances. This shows that where evidence has been corrupted or subverts the administration of justice – as has happened here – even a conviction following a guilty plea can be challenged.

But in reality, the implications of this go far beyond those directly involved. To start with, it has been estimated that VicPol faced legal costs of around $32,000 per day during the Royal Commission – that's $1.5 million a month to pay for a 100-strong legal team, paid for out of their own budget. But the costs to the public don't stop there. Gobbo was given around $2 million in her attempt to keep her identity a secret, and Victoria Police spent an additional $4.5 million to protect their source's safety – which ultimately ended in defeat in the High Court.

The impact is also being felt by people involved in other investigations, unsurprising given that VicPol has spent such a significant part of its budget on this one case. This means that resources that should have been spent elsewhere are being diverted to this investigation and inquiry – the Royal Commission was told that VicPol had a large team of barristers, solicitors and police officers dedicated to sorting through and evaluating thousands of pages of documentation related to Lawyer X's involvement as a human source over a significant number of criminal cases.

IN THE END . . .

No one can argue that this situation is anything other than extraordinary. Unprecedented.

It gives rise to serious questions around the integrity of the criminal justice system, not just in Victoria, but nationwide, as some have described this as the biggest legal crisis the country has seen.

Writing this in April 2020, I am, frankly, amazed Gobbo is still alive. And I'm not the only one. Gavan Ryan, a senior police officer and lead underworld investigator in Melbourne, gave evidence to the Commission. He stated that he was very concerned for her safety in 2006, and that 'I thought it was inevitable she would be killed'.

On the flip side, perhaps he is half right. Many criminals would probably pay for her security, given they now stand to benefit from the really serious legal issues this raises with their cases.

Gobbo is literally the best thing that has happened to some of them since they were convicted.

After this is all over, though, that may be a different story; when all the appeals have been heard, when she is no longer of use.

There's precedent, as Lawyer X is certainly not the first lawyer to have turned police informant, and people who choose to cross this line can pay a heavy price.

In 2016 mafia lawyer, 54-year-old Joseph Acquaro, was shot dead in Melbourne's inner north. Like Gobbo, Acquaro had represented some of Melbourne's most dangerous underworld characters, and also like Gobbo, had turned police informant. In 2018, Vincenzo Crupi was charged with Acquaro's murder, but at his pre-trial hearing in 2019 his defence lawyers were seeking access to the Royal Commission's findings, to determine if the police had any alternative suspects – which you would imagine they do, given Acquaro's risky decision to inform on such dangerous people. This would fit with the allegation that a year before he was murdered, the police told Acquaro that a senior mafia figure had put a bounty on his head, and he was therefore in grave danger.

The Commission's documents may either help an innocent man avoid being wrongly found guilty of murder, or alternatively provide the defence of a guilty man with a source of reasonable doubt.

And the web of deceit spreads further. At least three other lawyers were approached by VicPol to work with them, including one that has been murdered. Except Gobbo and Acquaro, their identities are suppressed. Other privileged informants include three county clerks or legal secretaries, and a legal adviser.

What I find totally intolerable is that, because of the failure of Victoria Police to manage their police informants appropriately – including making good decisions about who should be able to act as a source – it is possible that serious, violent offenders will now be released, putting the public in danger.

Yes, Gobbo gave the police a clear advantage in helping to dismantle Melbourne's criminal syndicates, but at what cost?

No one can be above the law, or above scrutiny.

There is a strong chance that, after the Royal Commission is concluded, Nicola Gobbo will be charged with criminal offences. And she is not alone. Simon Overland has conceded that members of VicPol may have acted illegally, and that police officers who used or were aware of her position as a privileged source may also face criminal charges, as all were perverting the course of justice through their association. This could mean senior members or ex-members of VicPol could go to prison, including Commissioner Graham Ashton (who is still with VicPol) and then-Assistant Commissioner Overland (who left the police in 2011), who were both allegedly complicit in the situation.

Legal and ethical considerations can't be ignored simply to cut corners to get results.

And where does it leave the families of the victims of soon-to-be-released offenders? To know that people who should be spending considerable amounts of time in prison may now be released because of poor police practice will be hard to reconcile for many intimately affected by these dangerous people.

Nicola Gobbo has a lot to answer for. I hope she is held to account by the same legal community she has failed so badly.

CONCLUSION

As we have seen, miscarriages of justice happen for many reasons, although common ones are police or prosecutorial misconduct and eyewitness misidentifications. But they aren't happening to 'other people', they are happening to people just like you and me.

Anyone can be accused of anything, and proving you are not guilty can be extremely challenging – sometimes the odds are stacked too heavily against you. And that problem is exacerbated when the accused is vulnerable – for example, they are known to police and may be an easy target or they have mental health problems.

DNA is a powerful tool to help exonerate the wrongly convicted, particularly as technologies have advanced so significantly recently, but as we have seen, once found guilty, people do not have a right to demand post-conviction testing. Added to this problem is the DNA testing backlog, and post-conviction tests are not going to be high up the priority order given the fact that there will be evidence from more recent serious and violent crimes to analyse.

Other issues arise when evidence focuses solely on guilt testing, to the exclusion of innocence testing.

Family and friends are often the biggest proponents of the wrongly convicted, but without significant financial means or training or experience in the workings of the criminal justice system, they can find themselves just shouting into the dark.

And more often than not, the legal world does not want to hear them.

You may be asking yourself why it even matters, as this is never going to happen to anyone you know. Well, I guarantee that everyone who has been wrongly convicted would say the same thing. That is why innocent people often waive their right to legal counsel early on, as they believe that the police will reach the correct conclusion. But sometimes that doesn't happen.

The effects of wrongful convictions impact us all. For those convicted, their lives stripped of dignity, the loss of relationships, wrecked finances, the almost impossibility of unpicking erroneous guilty verdicts, the lingering suspicion even if a conviction is over-turned. For the victims and their families, the lack of closure, the opening-up of old wounds through appeals, retrials, the constant delaying of justice, the turmoil of never knowing who was actually to blame. For society as a whole, these miscarriages of justice mean that the real criminals are still walking free, or may walk free in the case of Lawyer X. This is to say nothing of the financial cost of pros-ecuting, incarcerating, and compensating innocent people. And we can't ignore how miscarriages of justice can breed mistrust and fear of a system that we need to trust.

These are not isolated incidents that only touch a few lives.

As the cases in this book exemplify, without someone fighting in their corner, many of these miscarriages of justice would go unchallenged.

From all the cases of wrongful conviction I've looked at, they all have one thing in common – a champion. A hero or heroes who continue to fight for the accused, never giving up. And these champions offer us hope, as we need people willing to ask the tough questions of our criminal justice system and make sure the answers are transparent.

These champions could take the form of an innocence initiative, or other heavy hitter that has recognised the wrongs in a case – for example an ex-Attorney General or politician, an expert who has taken a special interest, or a member of the media. Examples of this are covered in this book, including Wayne Butler (chapter one) who spent 18 years in prison for murdering a woman on a beach in 1983. This was the first case 'solved' using DNA profiling, however a DNA expert, Professor Barry Boettcher, has raised significant concerns about the reliability of the evidence used to convict Butler, and continues to fight to help him clear his name. The Butler case also raises issues around systemic problems at forensic testing labs, and the confidence we can all have in the reliability of the results presented in court.

Without the intervention of legal expert Dr Bob Moles, Henry Keogh (chapter four) would still be in prison for the murder of his fiancée, as the result of the erroneous forensic evidence given by the forensic pathologist who undertook the deceased's post-mortem: A pathologist with no qualifications in pathology but an unshakable belief in his own abilities. Dr Moles, who is very well respected and a recognised expert in miscarriages of justice, saw the problems with the case and fought tirelessly to help Keogh clear his name.

Khalid Baker, whose case is covered in chapter six, sought the assistance of RMIT's Bridge of Hope Innocence Initiative to help clear his name after he was convicted of murdering a man at a party in 2005. Khalid spent 13 years in prison, even though his best friend admitted to being the last person to touch the victim before he fell 5.4 metres through a window, leading to catastrophic head trauma that resulted in his death two days later. The innocence initiative is now petitioning to have Khalid's conviction overturned, so that he will not always carry the stigma of having been convicted for murder.

This highlights why the work of innocence initiatives nationally and internationally is so important. The people working at and in association with these initiatives are committed to social justice, and are the white knights of the justice world.

One such group is The Bridge of Hope Foundation Inc., a Melbourne-based charity incorporated in 2002 working closely with Victorian-based RMIT University. The charity brings together criminal and civil lawyers to advise on potential wrongful convictions and social injustice under a management and reinvestigation control model formed by RMIT.

It has also established a wrongful convictions working group.

Its founder, John Walsh, who has evidence of a blatant and fraudulent act of prosecutorial misconduct (refer to section reviewing Rules of Disclosure), passionately told me, 'We must break the pipeline of disadvantage to prison, especially for our Aboriginal and Torres Strait Islander friends and young people generally.' For the vulnerable and underprivileged, The Bridge of Hope Foundation is their voice.

I am proud to be associated with such a group.

In other instances, the media takes an interest in a case, and often following a determined and dogged investigation, a journalist will find new information not available at the original trial. Sometimes, this information turns a case on its head. This happened with Kelvin Condren, discussed in chapter two, a young Aboriginal man found guilty of murdering his girlfriend in the small town of Mount Isa, Queensland. A coerced confession and forced witness statements, together with sloppy police work, resulted in Kelvin's wrongful conviction, overturned by a good investigative journalist digging until they found the truth – Condren had a water-tight alibi, he was in police custody at the time of the murder.

For Andrew Mallard, a case covered in chapter three, it took a politician and a journalist to join forces to ensure this wrongful conviction was overturned. In 1995, Mallard was simply a vulnerable person in the wrong place at the wrong time, and poor policing and a coerced police confession led to him spending 12 years in prison for a crime he did not commit, whilst the real perpetrator went on to kill again.

Nicola Gobbo (you know her better as Lawyer X) is the focus of the final miscarriages of justice covered in this book, as the cause rather than the victim. And as such she would do anything not to have drawn so much attention to herself. Until 2019, Gobbo's identity was a secret, because apart from being a police informer she was also a high-level criminal lawyer, having acted for many of Melbourne's most notorious underworld characters. When the case hit the media in 2019, people were shocked that Victoria Police would break every rule there is and allow a lawyer to inform on her clients even as she acted for them (a total breach of her duties to them). Now, because of the abuse of position, every case Gobbo has ever been involved with could be subject to review, and many people who are very likely guilty of serious and violent crimes can claim their cases have been tainted and their convictions are unsound as a result of her playing both sides. Some of them will be released on appeal because their conviction will be considered unsafe. This case represents multiple miscarriages of justice on a huge scale, and has rocked the legal and policing world in Victoria.

Together, these cases offer a snapshot of what can happen when people don't do their jobs properly or choose to work outside of the law.

The victims are real people, suffering at the hands of, at times, an unjust system. They have champions helping them fight for justice, but spare a thought for the others – innocent people in prison, without help, without hope.

Don't be depressed, though. These cases are awful and the stories sad. But, generally, our justice system works, and those who have committed crimes are sent to prison, and the innocent are exonerated. Just being open-minded to the fact that miscarriages of justice occur, and people are wrongfully convicted, helps to keep the system and those within it honest.

If you ever end up on a jury, be considered, be objective in your evaluation of the evidence, and remember, somebody's future is in your hands and there is every chance they may be an Andrew Mallard or a Khalid Baker.

Don't be blinded by science or powerful expert testimony; as we have seen, even the experts get it horribly wrong sometimes.

Sometimes there is really just smoke without fire.

And even if you are never formally involved in the criminal justice process, remember that the world is not black and white. We can all be more mindful when considering alleged criminality, and encourage the system to adapt to account for disadvantages (for example, cultural assistance for Indigenous people facing charges), extra training and resources for investigators to avoid tunnel vision, shifting cultural narratives around 'guilt' and 'innocence' to see the nuances, and the importance of organisations like innocence initiatives and the media as champions of the wrongfully accused.

This is particularly poignant as I write this final chapter in April 2020 – we are in the midst of the COVID-19 pandemic, and I am finishing this manuscript isolated in my home. I have very little contact with the outside world, and for the first time, like most other people, I am experiencing what it is like to be restricted to a very limited space. But I know soon, for me and the rest of the world trapped at home for our own safety, this will end.

Others are not so lucky. So spare a thought for those in prison – crowded conditions, poor sanitation, poor medical care, and many inmates have long-term medical conditions that weaken their immune systems. The conditions are rife for the virus to sweep through, literally a recipe for disaster. Then build in the effects of being cut off from their families, no visits, for some no contact at all. Psychologically this is very traumatising. The final weight some of them carry? That they are innocent.

I am already deeply troubled by the thought that wrongfully convicted persons languish in jail for months, years, or even decades, but at this time especially my heart breaks at the injustice of it. If ever we needed a reason to address the causes of miscarriages of justice, surely this is it?

Both professionally and personally I am deeply interested in and engaged with the workings of our criminal justice system. I wrote this book not just because the stories here need to be heard, but because I honestly believe that the only way to improve the system is to openly and directly address the flaws. We all have a part to play and a vested interest in ensuring our 'justice' system stands up to its name.

My last word: for all those working within the criminal justice system, to avoid miscarriages of justice from occurring, we should all aim to live by the moto: **Fight hard, but fight fair.**

EXPERT BIOGRAPHIES

TIM DORAN – BLOOD SPATTER

Tim Doran is an Assistant Chief of Police in Colorado and a retired Federal Bureau of Investigation Special Agent. Whilst assigned to the Evidence Response Team Unit at the FBI Laboratory, he authored the FBI Evidence Collection Manual and worked with educators and law enforcement crime scene investigation teams worldwide to develop these protocols. Educated at the United States Military Academy at West Point, Tim chose a career in law enforcement, which has spanned 29 years.

DR DIANA EADES – FORENSIC LINGUISTICS

Dr Diana Eades is a critical sociolinguist who has worked for more than four decades on communication by, with, and about Aboriginal speakers of English in the Australian legal system. In addition to publishing several books and many scholarly articles, she engages in training of judicial officers and other legal professionals, and has given expert evidence in courts and tribunals in three states and the Northern Territory.

DR CATRIONA HAVARD – WITNESS MISIDENTIFICATION BASED ON RACE

Dr Catriona Havard is a Senior Lecturer in the School of Psychology, The Open University. The main focus of her research is face recognition and eyewitness identification. Catriona has worked with police forces across the UK, investigating how accurate children, and older adults are at making identifications, and looked at ways to improve identification evidence. She has also examined other factors that influence face identification, such as the own-race bias. Her research has led to the development of new techniques to try to reduce the false identification rates that can lead to wrongful convictions.

SHAUN McCARTHY – THE BASIC COMPONENTS OF AN OFFENCE

Shaun is the Director of the University of Newcastle Legal Centre (UNLC) and Program Convenor of the Practical Legal Training Program at the University of Newcastle. He provides clinical supervision to law students at the UNLC and teaches in the Law School's Practice Program, Bachelor of Laws and Juris Doctor degrees. Shaun has acted in multiple high profile public interest cases at the UNLC, including the police shooting of Roni Levi on Bondi Beach and the inquiry into the detention of Cornelia Rau.

DR ROBERT MOLES – RULES OF DISCLOSURE AND THE RESPONSIBILITIES OF EXPERTS IN CRIMINAL TRIALS

Robert Moles is an Adjunct Principal Researcher at Flinders University. His first book, *Definition and Rule in Legal Theory* (1987), was internationally recognised as a major critique of Oxford-based legal theory. He is co-author of two books with Bibi Sangha. In addition he has authored two books that are cased-based analyses of wrongful convictions in South Australia. *A State of Injustice* (2004) details the circumstances and cases involving the Chief Forensic Pathologist in South Australia for over 25 years. *Losing Their Grip – the case of Henry Keogh* (2006) sets out the factors which led to the overturning of Mr Keogh's conviction. He has also developed the Networked Knowledge web site which provides extensive materials dealing with wrongful convictions from around the world.

ASSOCIATE PROFESSOR BIBI SANGHA – RULES OF DISCLOSURE

Associate Professor Bibi Sangha is an Adjunct Associate Professor in Law at Flinders University. She is the lead author of two major texts on wrongful convictions. *Forensic Investigations* (2010) provides a comparative analysis of the law and cases on wrongful convictions in Australia, Britain and Canada. *Criminal Appeals and the Rule of Law* (2015) discusses the development of the new right of appeal in Australia, which was the first major amendment to the law on criminal appeals in over 100 years. That development led to the overturning of the conviction of Henry Keogh after he had been imprisoned for over 20 years.

DR JODIE WARD – DNA PROFILING

Dr Jodie Ward is the Director of the Australian Facility for Taphonomic Experimental Research, Sydney, and an Associate Professor in the Centre for Forensic Science at University of Technology Sydney. In addition, she is the Forensic DNA Identification Specialist for the Forensic and Analytical Science Service at NSW Health Pathology, specialising in the use of nuclear and mitochondrial DNA testing for identifying compromised bone samples from modern and historical contexts. This unique joint appointment sees her lead the research, development, and application of forensic human identification techniques for missing persons casework in Australia.

ACKNOWLEDGMENTS

As ever, with any project of this nature, there are many people that have made invaluable contributions. Firstly, my great friend Duncan McNab, who was always on hand to correct my confusions (which are many), fill in gaps, and generally keep me on track. Likewise, Tim Watson-Munro has such an amazing mind for all things relating to criminal behaviour that he was a godsend, and always so supportive. I love our working lunches, and am thankful to count both Duncan and Tim amongst my closest friends and allies; the fact that they are both fantastic authors and willing to help when my writing skills let me down is just a bonus!

Dr Joel McGregor has again helped me, often by being the unfortunate victim for my outpourings when I hit a wall. But I do that for him too, so hopefully that keeps us square. My agent Lauren Miller has assisted me enormously throughout my career, and I would not have had the opportunities to be involved in so many great projects without her. My friend Tim Doran also agreed to contribute more of his wealth of policing knowledge to this book, for which I am extremely grateful.

I would also like to acknowledge John Walsh, of the Bridge of Hope Foundation Inc., who is always such a source of inspiration when it comes to addressing social justice issues. His passion inspires me, as he is constantly and tirelessly a voice for the voiceless, a true hero, and I am grateful to him for allowing me to be involved with some of the BOH's important work.

I can't thank Professor Barry Boettcher enough in regards to helping me work through the intricacies of the DNA evidence in regards to Celia Douty's murder, for which Wayne Butler remains convicted. I don't know if Butler is guilty, but Barry opened my eyes to some very serious issues in the handling of DNA evidence.

The team at Pan Macmillan were again amazing, including my publisher Cate Blake, senior editor Danielle Walker and publicist Charlotte Howells, as well as my copy editor James Smith, and of course Ingrid Ohlsson as Director of Non-Fiction for again showing faith in my literary abilities. You all did such a great job of helping me shape the narratives and improve the flow, so thank you all.

Last but clearly not least, I want to give a heartfelt thanks to those who contributed the expert additions to this book, as readers have told me these are some of their favourite elements: Tim Doran for educating us in the science of blood spatter; Dr Jodie Ward for detailing the process of DNA profiling; Dr Diana Eades for sharing her expertise in forensic linguistics; Shaun McCarthy for outlining the basic components of an offence; Dr Bob Moles and Associate Professor Bibi Sangha for sharing their legal knowledge in relation to rules of disclosure, as well as Bob contributing to the discussion around the responsibilities of experts in criminal trials; and Dr Catriona Havard for elucidating the hazards of identification where race is a factor.

Cold Case Investigations
Dr Xanthé Mallett

From the disappearance of the Beaumont children to the abduction of William Tyrrell to the double murder of Karlie Pearce-Stevenson and her daughter Khandalyce, Xanthé is determined to expose the truth to maximise dignity for both deceased victims and those left behind.

Xanthé talks to experts to uncover the how's and why's of tragic murders and haunting disappearances. Along the way readers will also be introduced to new forensic techniques and scientific methods that could – or did – help move the case forward.

Cold Case Investigations covers mostly murders or suspected murders – such as Ashley Coulston, Mr Cruel and Ivan Milat – with the victims as the focus. Not only because, criminologically speaking, the more you can learn about your victim the more you can extrapolate about the person who killed or abducted them, but also because they deserve their stories to be told. They deserve for people to know their names. They shouldn't just be someone's victim.